THE One & Only Smoothies, Shakes and Juices Cookbook

THE
One & Only
Smoothies, Shakes and Juices Cookbook

METRO BOOKS
New York

METRO BOOKS
New York

An Imprint of Sterling Publishing
387 Park Avenue South
New York, NY 10016

METRO BOOKS and the distinctive Metro Books logo are trademarks of Sterling Publishing Co., Inc

Copyright © 2012 Pulp Media Limited

This 2012 edition published by Metro Books by arrangement with Pulp Media Limited

Written by: Wendy Sweetser
Project Editors: Catherine Knight and Helen Caldon
Art Director: Susi Martin
Publisher: James Tavendale
Photography: All photography by Ian Garlick with the exception of pages
2, 5, 10, 12, 22, 24, 40, 54, 74, 88, 100, 106, 108, 122, 136, 152, 168, 174, 176, 190, 211, 229, 245, 256 (www.shutterstock.com),

Every effort has been made to credit photographers and copyright-holders. If any have been overlooked, Pulp Media will be pleased to make the necessary corrections in subsequent editions.

ISBN 978-1-4351-4491-0

For information about custom editions, special sales, and premium and corporate purchases, please contact Sterling Special Sales at 800–805–5489 or specialsales@sterlingpublishing.com

Manufactured in China

10 9 8 7 6 5 4 3 2 1

www.sterlingpublishing.com

Contents

Foreword

As around 95% of the nutrients in fruit and vegetables are to be found in their juice, homemade smoothies, shakes, and juices aren't just refreshing and satisfying to drink, they also form an important part of a balanced diet. Making drinks from fruit and vegetables is an easy and very enjoyable way of upping your daily intake of body-boosting minerals and vitamins, not least because it's you who decides what goes into them.

This book contains 100 easy-to-follow recipes for making healthy, delicious drinks using a rainbow of different-colored fruits and vegetables, some of which—such as apples, peaches, and pears— are everyday favorites, while others you may be less familiar with. So, if dragon fruit, pomelos, or Sharon fruit have caught your eye in your local greengrocers but you don't know what to do with them, now is your chance to give them a try.

Opening a carton or bottle of a ready-made drink doesn't compare with the feel-good factor you get from pouring a tall glass of something you've made yourself—and you won't have any trouble persuading all the family to help whip up their favorite smoothies and shakes too.

Tips for making smoothies, shakes, and juices

Do I need special equipment to make the drinks in this book?

Strictly speaking, while smoothies and shakes are made by blending the pulp and juice of whole fruit and vegetables together in a juicer (usually with a dairy product such as milk, yogurt, or buttermilk), juices are purely the liquid produced after putting the fruit and vegetables through a special machine that extracts their juice, separating it from the pulp and less easily digestible bits, which is then discarded.

There are a wide variety of these juicing machines on the market, but the sturdier, more powerful ones needed to pulverize tougher fruits and vegetables are expensive to buy and often too large to fit easily into most peoples' kitchen cupboards. So in this book I've made all the drinks by blending a mixture of fresh fruit or vegetables with the most popular ready-prepared juices, meaning all the recipes can be made in a standard domestic juicer or by using an immersion blender. However, if you do own a juice extractor or want to invest in one, you can prepare the orange, apple, pineapple, tomato, grapefruit, and other basic juices I've used in the recipes yourself.

Which fruits and vegetables are more suitable for making drinks, and how do I prepare them?

Any fruit or vegetable can be pulverized on its own to make a drink, but while a glass of orange or pineapple juice might look and taste delicious, most people — especially children—wouldn't find a glass of pure beets, celery, or parsnip juice so appealing.

Combining different fruits and vegetables that have complementary flavors is the key to making successful drinks—and it is also an excellent way of introducing vegetables such as spinach and into

into the diet of fussy eaters by hiding them amongst other more popular flavors!

When making drinks in a juicer or by using an immersion blender, the fruit needs to be prepared first. Some fruits and vegetables can be chucked into the blender skin and all, but some may need a little preparation first to prevent damage to your juicer and to create a smoother drink.

Fruits with tough or bitter skins need to be peeled before juicing; some can easily be removed, but others, on fruits such as peaches and apricots, might need a little help. Just as you would a tomato before skinning it, put the fruit in a heatproof bowl and pour over sufficient boiling

water to cover them. Leave them to stand for 1 minute, then tip them into a colander to drain off the water and rinse them under cold running water until cool enough to handle. The skins should come away quite easily now.

Fruits that contain inedible elements such as stalks and pips need to be cored and these less palatable bits removed and discarded.

Tough vegetables such as sweet potato, squash, or broccoli can be liquidized but they need cooking and roughly mashing first so that they will combine evenly with other, softer ingredients. Each recipe in this book gives details of how you should prepare such fruits and vegetables when they feature in the drinks.

If you use a juice extractor to prepare your own juices, fruits and vegetables— even organic ones— need to be washed thoroughly. You will still need to prepare the ingredients, such as by discarding any hard stalks or stones from fruits like peaches, cherries, and mangos, but apple cores, melon seeds, and celery leaves are softer and can be left in and will be filtered off as pulp by the machine. Before loading up a juicer, you should cut the fruit and vegetable flesh into pieces that are small enough to fit comfortably down the feeder tube of the machine, and only remove the skin if it is tough and

dry and likely to cause damage to your machine's workings. Watermelon, for example, has a soft, thin skin that can be left on, whereas an ogen melon's skin is thick and hard and needs to be removed.

How many servings will the recipes make?

In the majority of cases, I've given the amount each recipe serves, but this should only be taken as a guide as the size of fruit and vegetables used and how much juice or pulp they contain will determine the volume of the finished drink. Some drinks also thicken on standing, so any that you feel are too thick can be diluted with water, milk, or more juice. An average serving for an adult is 200ml (7fl oz), but for children it will depend on their age and appetite.

What do I do if a drink separates or is too frothy?

Pulverizing fruit and vegetables in a juicer pushes the starch out of the flesh and, if left to stand, this may cause the juice to separate. It can also create quite a head of froth on the drink and you might feel neither a separated drink nor a frothy one looks very appetising. However, a quick stir-up with a spoon or balloon whisk and your juice will be back to looking as it should and any excess froth can simply be spooned or strained off. Alternatively, serve the juice with a straw so it can be drunk from the bottom up. Most drinks are also best consumed when freshly made, as the longer they're kept the more vitamins they will lose and, if exposed to the air for too long, juices containing apples and bananas can start to discolor and turn brown as the fruit begins to oxidise.

Should I strain drinks before serving?

Children are notorious for not liking "drinks with bits in", and whether you strain drinks to remove raspberry or kiwi fruit pips, tiny flecks of skin from fruits such as cherries, nectarines, or blueberries, is very much down to personal taste. While it's a good idea to skin fruits such as peaches and apricots, it's not practical with small fruits such as cherries or grapes, and when blended the skins of these fruits won't break down completely. To ensure your drinks are as smooth and silky as possible, blend the ingredients together for 1–2 minutes to pulverize any lumps of fruit and then push the juice through a fine sieve. Press down on the pulp with the back of a spoon to extract as much liquid as possible before pouring the drink into glasses.

Can I only make juices with fresh fruit?

Canned, bottled, frozen, and reconstituted dried fruit can all be used, as well as fresh. When using canned or bottled fruit, try to choose those in fruit juice rather than syrup, if possible. When buying fresh fruit, the riper it is, the better, as it will have a greater concentration of antioxidants and will be sweeter and more fragrant. Avoid produce that's blemished or past its best, as its levels of nutrients and amount of juice it contains will have diminished.

Smoothies

Smoothies

Just saying the word "smoothie" seduces you into wanting to drink one and I hope the recipes I've devised for this book will tempt you into making your own. Traditionally made by blending fruit or vegetables with dairy products such as milk, yogurt, cream, or buttermilk, they are thicker than straight juices and wonderfully satisfying. They can also be quite calorific if you overdo the dairy fat content, so where I've specified milk, this can be whole milk, semi-skim or skim, and similarly you can substitute low-fat versions of yogurt and cream.

If you follow a dairy-free diet, soya milk and soya yogurt can be substituted in all the recipes that use cow's milk, plus other non-dairy products like almond milk, coconut milk, or water can be used as well.

Golden glow

INGREDIENTS
*4 fresh apricots or 8 apricot halves canned
   in fruit juice*
½ cup (150ml) orange juice
½ cup (150ml) almond milk
½ cup (150ml) natural soya yogurt

TO SERVE
Toasted flaked almonds

MAKES
2.4 cups (600ml)

If you need to avoid dairy products, smoothies can often seem a treat that's out of reach, but to make this drink I've used almond milk instead of cow's milk and soya yogurt, so you can indulge as much as you wish. Made by grinding whole almonds with water, commercially produced almond milk is often enriched with calcium and vitamins. It is also low in saturated fat and contains no cholesterol or lactose. If all that makes it sound like a modern convenience food created in a laboratory, almond milk has actually been around since the Middle Ages. From western Europe to east Asia, it was a staple in many kitchens before the days of refrigeration. Because cow's milk spoiled so quickly, particularly in warm climates, it was churned into butter as soon as the cow had been milked, while almonds and water provided an early version of long-life milk.

1 If using fresh apricots, peel them first, following the instructions on page 15, then halve them and remove and discard the stones.

2 Put the apricots in a juicer, add the orange juice and blend until smooth.

3 Add the almond milk and yogurt and blend again until evenly combined.

4 Pour into glasses and serve sprinkled with toasted flaked almonds.

Apricot and tangerine zinger

Smaller than oranges and with slightly flattened tops, tangerines are always a favorite with children as their loose skins makes them easy to peel and divide into segments. Thought to originate from China, where they have been grown for thousands of years and where they are known as mandarins, tangerines were renamed after the port of Tangiers in north Africa, where the fruits were first imported into Europe from the East. Tangerines are a good source of vitamin C, folate for building healthy cells, and beta carotene.

1 If using fresh apricots, peel them first, following the instructions on page 15, then halve them and remove and discard the stones.

2 Peel the banana and cut it into chunks.

3 Put the apricots and banana in a juicer, add the tangerine juice and blend until smooth. Add the yogurt and milk and blend again until creamy.

4 Pour into glasses and serve at once with apricot and banana slices threaded onto cocktail sticks or small skewers to enjoy with the drinks.

INGREDIENTS

4 fresh apricots or 8 apricot halves canned in fruit juice
1 banana
½ cup (115ml) freshly squeezed tangerine juice
½ cup (150ml) apricot or peach yogurt
¾ cup (200ml) milk

TO SERVE

Apricot and banana slices

MAKES

3 cups (700ml)

Avocado and peanut silk

Avocados are one of nature's wonder foods that promise to look after you at every stage of your life. So nutritious are avocados that in Israel, where they grow prolifically, mothers mash the flesh and feed it to toddlers and babies. As we mature into adults avocados are reputed to help fight many types of cancer, plus they lower cholesterol and their high levels of folate regulate blood pressure and promote a healthy heart. And, if that wasn't enough, by the time we reach our senior years, the trusty avocado is there to protect our eyes. Containing more carotenoid lutein than any other regularly eaten fruit, avocados help guard against macular degeneration, cataracts and other age-related eye problems.

1 Halve the avocado, remove the stone, then peel and chop the flesh.

2 Peel the cucumber, cut it in half lengthways and remove the seeds. Chop the flesh into chunks.

3 Put the avocado, cucumber, lime juice, and peanut butter in a juicer. Add half the apple juice and blend until smooth.

4 Add the remaining apple juice, milk, and cilantro and blend again.

5 Pour into glasses and serve with a few small cilantro leaves and a dusting of paprika on each drink.

INGREDIENTS

1 ripe avocado
¼ cucumber
Juice of 2 limes
4 tbsp smooth or crunchy peanut butter
1¼ cups (300ml) apple juice
1 cup (225ml) milk
1 tbsp chopped fresh cilantro

TO SERVE

Extra cilantro leaves and paprika

MAKES

3¾ cups (900ml)

Banana, strawberry, and goji berry smoothie

The banana plant is one of the oldest cultivated plants in the world and, despite its size, it is classified botanically as a herb. Native to south and southeast Asia, hundreds of different varieties of banana are now grown in over 100 countries — short and stumpy, long and slender, or with thick or thin skins that are yellow or red. Composed mainly of sugars and fibers, bananas are a good source of slow-release energy, making them the perfect breakfast food when you have a busy morning ahead.

1 Peel the banana and cut it into chunks.

2 Hull the strawberries and quarter or halve any large fruits. Cut the peel and pith away from the orange and divide the flesh into segments.

3 Put the banana, strawberries, orange, goji berry juice, and strawberry yogurt in a juicer and blend until smooth.

4 Add the pineapple juice and blend again.

5 Pour into glasses and serve, sprinkling a few goji berries on top of each drink.

INGREDIENTS

1 banana
5oz (150g) strawberries
1 large orange
¼ cup (50ml) goji berry juice
½ cup (150ml) strawberry yogurt
1¼ cups (300ml) pineapple juice

TO SERVE

Dried goji berries

MAKES

3¾ cups (900ml)

Red jewel

Beets may not be everyone's favorite salad ingredient but blended in a smoothie with sweet fruits like pears they lose much of their earthy flavor that is prevalent when they are eaten on their own. Full of blood-cleansing minerals and vitamins, beets also help overcome fatigue when you've had a trying and exhausting day. Be warned, though, if you discover you like the taste of beets in a drink and start juicing or smoothie-ing it regularly, their vibrant red color will pass straight through you—so don't be alarmed when you go to the loo!

1 Peel the beets, place on a plate and cut into small chunks so you don't lose any of the juice.

2 Twist the stalk off the pear, cut it into quarters, remove the core and peel away the skin.

3 Cut the peel and pith away from the orange and divide the flesh into segments.

4 Put the beets, pear, and orange in a juicer, add the cranberry juice, apple, and raspberry juice and blend until smooth. Add the buttermilk and blend again until it is mixed in.

5 Pour into glasses and serve.

INGREDIENTS

4oz (115g) cooked beets
1 pear
1 orange
½ cup (150ml) cranberry juice
½ cup (150ml) apple and raspberry juice
½ cup (115ml) buttermilk

MAKES

3½ cups (800ml)

Berry good

Bananas are one of the best ingredients you can add to a smoothie, as not only do they add sweetness but they also work well in pretty much any combination of fruits. In this recipe they are mixed with raspberries and blueberries to give a thick, creamy consistency that makes a very satisfying drink. The smoothie can be strained to remove the raspberry seeds, or not—as you prefer—and it's quite fun to float a few small edible flowers on top of each drink when you serve them. I've used the pretty blue flowers from the herb borage, but substitute whatever edible flowers are available.

INGREDIENTS

1 banana
6oz (175g) raspberries
6oz (175g) blueberries
1¼ cups (300ml) apple juice
½ cup (150ml) strawberry yogurt

TO SERVE

Borage or other small edible flowers

MAKES

3¾ cups (900ml)

1 Peel the banana and cut it into chunks.

2 Put the banana, raspberries, and blueberries in a juicer, add the apple juice and blend until smooth.

3 Strain, if preferred, and return the fruit purée to the rinsed-out juicer. Add the strawberry yogurt and blend again until it is mixed in.

4 Pour into glasses and serve decorated with small edible flowers.

Blue heaven

Dubbed the "purple pearl of the Amazon", the dark violet, almost black, açai (pronounced "ah-sai-ee") berry is native to the impenetrable rainforests around the Amazon river and its tributaries. The berries have firm flesh and a robust stone and grow in large bunches that hang from the branches of tall, leafy palms. Tribes indigenous to the forests harvest the fruit daily and send it downriver to be sold in markets from where the berries are processed to a thick purée. On its own, this is quite bitter and acidic but when sweetened with a little honey or sugar it makes a superlatively healthy addition to drinks, ice creams, or sauces, as the berries contain jaw-dropping amounts of antioxidants and other nutrients.

1 Pull the stalks off the blackcurrants and the cherries and remove the stones from the cherries.

2 Cut the peel and pith away from the orange and divide the flesh into segments.

3 Put the blackcurrants, cherries, and orange segments in a juicer, add the blueberry juice, acai berry juice, honey, and yogurt and blend until smooth.

4 Pour into glasses and serve each drink with extra sprigs of blackcurrants.

MERINGUES

6oz (175g) blackcurrants
5oz (150g) black cherries
1 orange
1¼ cups (300ml) blueberry juice
¼ cup (50ml) açai berry juice
1–2 tbsp honey, or to taste
4 tbsp natural yogurt

TO SERVE

Extra sprigs of blackcurrants

MAKES

3¾ cups (900ml)

Banana, fig, and strawberry boost

INGREDIENTS
1 banana
2 figs
4oz (115g) strawberries
2 tsp lemon juice
1¼ cups (300ml) soya milk
4 tbsp soya yogurt
2 tbsp maple syrup

TO SERVE
Sunflower seeds

SERVES
3½ cups (800ml)

We hear a lot about that apple in the Garden of Eden, but if Adam and Eve were designer-clad in fig leaves after eating it, presumably figs were another indulgence on offer. As with so many fruits that date back to ancient times, figs are prized both for their medicinal and culinary properties. They have one of the highest levels of calcium of all fruits and are amongst the most highly alkaline, which balances acidity levels in the body. It's best to peel the figs to make this juice, but the soft seeds break down when blended so they don't need sieving out. Also, if you prefer to use cow's milk and yogurt, these can replace the soya.

1 Peel and chop the banana into chunks. Trim the stalks off the figs and cut away the peel. Hull the strawberries and cut any large fruits into halves or quarters.

2 Place the banana, figs, and strawberries in a juicer and add the lemon juice, soya milk, yogurt, and maple syrup. Blend until smooth.

3 Pour into glasses and serve with a sprinkling of sunflower seeds on each drink.

Blackcurrant, pomegranate, and yogurt smoothie

INGREDIENTS

6oz (175g) blackcurrants

½ cup (150ml) pomegranate juice

½ cup (150ml) black cherry or blackberry yogurt

¾ cup (200ml) milk

3 tbsp maple syrup

TO SERVE

Seeds from a fresh pomegranate

SERVES

3 cups (700ml)

Blackcurrants may not have the "wow" factor of other more fashionable berries and currants, but if ever a fruit deserved to be dubbed a "superfood", it is the humble blackcurrant. One of the healthiest fruits, blackcurrants top the nutrients league, scoring higher than favorites like apples and strawberries or bananas and mangoes. And, when it comes to antioxidants, those vital natural compounds that help protect the body from a range of illnesses from heart disease to cancer, blackcurrants are in a class of their own.

1 Pull the blackcurrants off their stalks and place in a juicer.

2 Add the pomegranate juice and yogurt and blend until smooth.

3 Add the milk and maple syrup and blend again until combined.

4 Pour into glasses and serve with a few pomegranate seeds sprinkled over each drink.

Blueberry and banana cooler

Blueberries might not be the prettiest or most exciting-looking fruit, but when it comes to promoting good health, these unassuming little blue-black balls are in a league of their own. Loaded with antioxidants designed to boost our immune systems and fight off disease, blueberries are valuable for keeping bladder problems like cystitis at bay and ensuring our blood courses smoothly through our veins. One group of these antioixidants—flavenoids—boosts the production of collagen in the skin, helping keep us looking younger for longer. If there's a better reason for making the most of blueberries, I've yet to hear it!

1 Peel the banana and chop it into chunks.

2 Place the banana in a juicer and add the blueberries and apple juice. Blend until smooth.

3 Add the fromage frais and blend again briefly until evenly combined.

4 Pour into glasses and serve with a few extra blueberries dropped into the smoothie.

INGREDIENTS

1 small banana
8oz (225g) blueberries
1¼ cups (300ml) apple juice
2oz (50g) natural fromage frais

TO SERVE

Extra blueberries

MAKES

2½ cups (600ml)

Cherry nice

This smoothie is quite thick so, if necessary, dilute it by adding still mineral water to achieve the consistency you require. It will also separate if left to stand, but a quick stir-up with a fork or a balloon whisk will bring it smoothly back together. As both cherries and their juice are quite sweet, it shouldn't be necessary to add honey, maple syrup, or sugar but, once again, this is down to personal taste.

1 Pull the stalks off the cherries and remove the pits.

2 Cut the apple into quarters, remove the core and peel.

3 Put the cherries and apple in a juicer, add the lime juice and half the cherry juice and blend until smooth.

4 Add the remaining cherry juice and coconut milk and blend again until combined.

5 Pour into glasses and decorate each drink with a sprinkling of desiccated coconut and extra fresh cherries.

INGREDIENTS

11oz (300g) red cherries
1 apple
Juice of 1 lime
1¼ cups (300ml) cherry juice
4 tbsp coconut milk

TO SERVE

Desiccated coconut and fresh cherries

MAKES

3½ cups (800ml)

Cherry and apricot smoothie

The young George Washington might have missed out on a juicy bowl of cherries when he cut down his father's tree but perhaps he discovered later in life just how sweet and tempting these delicious little fruit can be. Easy to transport and even easier to eat, cherries are perfect for popping into lunch boxes and picnic baskets. They're excellent in smoothies, too, and are full of good things. One of the few foods to contain a significant amount of melatonin, this antioxidant ensures a peaceful night's sleep, helps cope with jetlag, and keeps your heart beating regularly. Cherries are also known as "brain food", keeping your memory sharp and those senior moments at bay.

1 If using fresh apricots, skin them following the instructions on page 15, then halve them and remove and discard the stones.

2 Put the apricot halves and pitted cherries in a juicer, add the milk and yogurt and blend until smooth.

3 Strain, if preferred, to sieve out any flecks of cherry skin, pour into glasses and serve with extra fresh cherries.

INGREDIENTS

4 fresh apricots or 8 canned apricot halves
6oz (175g) fresh cherries, stalks removed and pitted or 5oz (150g) canned cherries (drained weight)
¾ cup (200ml) milk
½ cup (150ml) natural yogurt

TO SERVE

Extra cherries

MAKES

3 cups (700ml)

Velvet underground

It's always nice to know that something we look on as an indulgence is actually good for us too, and happily chocolate falls into that category. As it is produced from cocoa beans, chocolate contains plant nutrients so is packed with natural antioxidants that help protect against heart disease and lower blood pressure—although most of us don't need a scientist to tell us we feel more relaxed after a bit of chocolate therapy. The darker the chocolate, the higher proportion of cocoa solids it contains, so the better it is for us but, as with most good things, moderation is the name of the game—so put that second bar back in the cupboard!

1 Cut a small wedge from the orange and rub it around the rim of each glass. Spread out the chocolate on a plate and dip the rims of the glasses in the chocolate until they are coated in an even layer.

2 Peel and cut the pith away from the rest of the orange and divide into segments.

3 Twist the stalk off the pear, quarter, remove the core and peel.

4 Put the orange segments, pear, evaporated milk, and chocolate milk in a juicer and blend until smooth. Pour into the glasses and serve with an extra dusting of chocolate on each drink.

INGREDIENTS
1 orange
2oz (50g) finely grated dark chocolate
1 pear
½ cup (150ml) evaporated milk
1 cup (225ml) chocolate milk

TO SERVE
Extra grated chocolate

MAKES
3 cups (700ml)

Apple, cinnamon, and ginger glow

INGREDIENTS

1 apple
1 banana
Small knob of root ginger
4fl oz (115ml) orange juice
½ tsp ground cinnamon
½ cup (150ml) milk
½ cup (150ml) natural yogurt

MAKES

2½ cups (600ml)

Cinnamon and ginger are both regarded as "sweet spices" as their warm, mellow flavor adds its own special magic to sweet as well as savory dishes. They also contribute a comforting glow to a drink, as in this winter warmer of a smoothie that's perfect for helping to keep out the cold when the temperature plummets. If jars of fresh ginger purée are available, you can use 1 teaspoon purée instead of grating or chopping root ginger.

1 Quarter the apple, cut it into quarters and remove the core and skin.

2 Peel the banana and cut it into chunks. Peel the ginger and fine chop or grate it–you need about 1 teaspoon.

3 Put the apple, banana, ginger, orange juice, cinnamon, and milk in a juicer and blend until smooth. Add the yogurt and blend again until combined.

4 Pour into glasses and serve.

Blueberry and melon buzz

Cultured milk products have been around for thousands of years and we're as aware today of the healthy benefits to be derived from yogurt as the ancient civilizations of India and Persia were all those millennia ago. Easier to digest than milk, yogurt promotes the growth of healthy bacteria in the colon and is a rich source of calcium. Its tangy flavor and creamy texture work well in a smoothie, balancing the sweetness of fruit and thickening the drink, but if you find its flavor a bit too sharp, a little clear honey drizzled into the juicer will satisfy even the sweetest tooth.

INGREDIENTS
½ cantaloupe melon
3oz (75g) blueberries
½ cup (150ml) pineapple juice
¾ cup (200ml) natural yogurt
1–2 tbsp honey, or to taste

MAKES
3 cups (700ml)

1 Scoop out the seeds from the melon, peel off the skin and chop the flesh into chunks.

2 Put the melon and blueberries in a juicer, add the pineapple juice and blend until smooth.

3 Add the yogurt and honey and blend again until combined. Pour into glasses and serve.

Apple, orange, and cranberry smoothie

INGREDIENTS
2 apples
1 large orange
1 banana
1 cup (225ml) cranberry juice
½ cup (150ml) natural yogurt

MAKES
3¾ cups (900ml)

One of the few fruits that is too hard and too sharp to eat raw, most of us enjoy cranberries in the form of a drink, the vivid scarlet berries adding visual appeal to a sparkling juice or a creamy smoothie. Cranberries are also another of "nature's best friends", providing us with a wealth of nutrients and crammed full of antioxidants that fight to keep us healthy. Clinically proven to help block urinary tract infections, many scientists feel that when it comes fighting disease they've barely scratched the surface of the cranberry's potential, and research into how it might help prevent heart disease and different forms of cancer are very much on-going.

1 Cut the apples into quarters, peel and remove the cores.

2 Cut the peel and pith away from the orange and divide the flesh into segments, discarding any pips.

3 Peel the banana and cut into chunks.

4 Put the apples, orange segments, and banana into a juicer, add the cranberry juice and yogurt and blend until smooth.

5 Skim or strain off any froth, if preferred, then pour into glasses and serve.

Two melon and strawberry smoothie

Piel de sapo sounds a romantic name for a melon until you discover it translates from the original Spanish as "toad skin"! These long melons, shaped like footballs, have tough green skin speckled with brown and gold spots—hence their name—but inside the flesh is pale yellow, sweet, and fragrant. Widely grown in Spain and mainly available in Europe at present, if your local supermarket doesn't stock these melons, a wedge of fully ripe honeydew works equally well in this refreshing smoothie.

1 Peel the wedges of melon and scoop out the seeds. Chop the flesh into chunks.

2 Put the flesh of both melons in a juicer, add the apple juice and strawberry yogurt and blend until smooth.

3 Half-fill glasses with crushed ice, pour the smoothie over the ice, stir, and serve.

INGREDIENTS

5oz (150g) wedge of honeydew melon or piel de sapo melon
1½lb (700g) wedge of watermelon
½ cup (115ml) apple juice
4 tbsp strawberry yogurt

TO SERVE

Crushed ice

MAKES

3 cups (700ml)

Halloween scream

INGREDIENTS

*6oz (175g) cooked pumpkin or butternut
    squash flesh*

1 banana

*1 pineapple ring, fresh or canned in fruit
    juice*

½ cup (150ml) pineapple juice

1¼ cups (300ml) orange juice

MAKES

3¾ cups (800ml)

At Halloween you can use some of the flesh you've scooped out of your pumpkin lantern to make this smoothie, but cooked butternut squash works equally well during the rest of the year, as does canned, unsweetened pumpkin. Harry Potter introduced us all to the idea of turning pumpkin into "wizard juice" and a glass of this is a fun way for children to celebrate Halloween. Let's not forget the moms and dads, however, as not only is pumpkin a storehouse of nutrients like carotenoids that help hold back the ageing process, it's also a natural aphrodisiac for both men and women. Enough said!

1 Mash the pumpkin or squash flesh coarsely. Peel the banana and cut it into chunks.

2 Chop the pineapple into small pieces.

3 Put the pumpkin or squash, banana, and pineapple in a juicer and add the pineapple juice. Blend until smooth.

4 Add the orange juice and blend again. Pour into glasses and serve at once.

Kiwi, apricot, and mint crush

Apricots have been grown in Armenia since ancient times, so long in fact that the fruit trees are believed to have originated there. From Armenia they travelled both east to China and west to Europe, with settlers eventually taking them across the Atlantic to the New World. Loose-stoned with velvet-soft skin that shades from golden yellow to blush pink, apricots don't just look good, they're good for you too. Low in calories compared to other fruit— 3 apricots only clock up about 50 calories—and they are packed with just about every nutrient you can think of. Vitamins A, C, and E, potassium, iron, beta carotene, and antioxidants like lycopene, to name just a few, putting apricots in a league of their own.

1 Rub the rim of each glass with the lime wedge and dip it in the superfine sugar to coat in an even layer.

2 Peel and chop the kiwi fruit.

3 If using fresh apricots, peel them following the instructions on page 15, then halve them and remove and discard the stones.

4 Put the kiwi fruit, apricot halves, lime juice, mint, and half the grape juice in a juicer and blend until smooth.

5 Add the rest of the grape juice, the honey, and yogurt and blend again until evenly mixed. Pour into glasses and serve.

INGREDIENTS

Lime wedge
Superfine sugar
2 kiwi fruit
2 fresh apricots or 4 canned apricot halves
2 tbsp fresh lime juice
1 tbsp chopped fresh mint
1¼ cups (300ml) white grape juice
2 tbsp honey
4 tbsp natural yogurt

MAKES

3 cups (700ml)

Mango and lime lassi

Lassi is India's answer to a smoothie, a traditional drink from the Punjab region that was originally just natural yogurt blended with water, spices, and salt. The perfect cooling antidote to a spicy curry, a sweet alternative to salty lassi is also made where the salt is replaced with jaggery, a raw sugar that is made from cane sugar and coconut palm sap and has a soft, crumbly texture. More recently fruit lassis have become popular and, as a mango-loving nation, those made with the fragrant fruit are the number one favorite. Delicious enjoyed on on a warm, sunny day.

1 Peel the mangoes and cut the flesh away from the fibrous center stone.

2 Chop the mango flesh and place it in a juicer with the lime juice, honey, and yogurt. Blend until smooth.

3 Add three-quarters of the mineral water and blend again. Check the consistency of the lassi and add more water to bring it to the right consistency, as necessary.

4 Pour into glasses and serve each drink sprinkled with ground cardamom.

INGREDIENTS

2 ripe medium-sized mangoes

Juice of 1 lime

2 tsp clear honey

1¼ cups (300ml) natural yogurt

about 1¾ cups (400ml) still mineral water

TO SERVE

Ground cardamom

MAKES

About 4¼ cups (1 litre)

Mango, yogurt, and peach smoothie

INGREDIENTS

1 medium mango, about 11oz (300g)
   unpeeled weight
1 yellow-fleshed peach
½ cup (150ml) natural yogurt
½ tsp vanilla extract
¾ cup (200ml) milk

MAKES

2½ cups (600ml)

Some smoothies thicken on standing and this is one of them, so if you make it ahead you'll probably need to dilute it to a drinkable consistency with extra milk or still mineral water. You can buy ready-flavored vanilla yogurt if you don't have a bottle of essence in your store cupboard, but some vanilla yogurts are quite sweet and mixed with a super-ripe mango and luscious peach you may find you need to sharpen the finished drink with a squeeze or two of fresh lime juice.

1 Peel the mango and cut the flesh away from the fibrous center stone.

2 Peel the peach following the instructions on page 15, then cut it into quarters, removing and discarding the stone.

3 Put the mango and peach in a juicer and add the yogurt, vanilla, and milk. Blend until smooth.

4 Pour into glasses and serve.

Passion fruit, mango, and buttermilk smoothie

Traditionally buttermilk was the liquid left over when milk was churned for butter and cream. Today's buttermilk is factory produced with a culture of lactic acid bacteria being added to cow's milk to thicken it and give buttermilk its distinctive flavor. Used with fruit to make a smoothie, its sharpness contrasts well with the sweetness of the fruit, but if you find this too tart for your taste, increase the quantity of honey or replace the lemon juice with water.

1 Halve the passion fruit and scoop out the seeds and pulp into a small pan. Add the lemon juice and simmer for 2 minutes. Push through a sieve to separate the seeds from the pulp. Put the pulp in a juicer, reserving a few of the seeds to sprinkle on top of the drinks.

2 Peel the mango and cut the flesh away from the stone. Chop and add to the juicer with the apple juice and honey. Blend until smooth.

3 Add the buttermilk to the fruit in the juicer and blend again until combined.

4 Pour into glasses and serve with a few passion fruit seeds sprinkled over each drink.

INGREDIENTS

4 passion fruit
Juice of ½ lemon
1 medium mango
½ cup (150ml) apple juice
2 tbsp honey
1¼ cups (300ml) buttermilk

MAKES

3¼ cups (800ml)

Heaven in a glass

INGREDIENTS
1 banana
2 tbsp smooth peanut butter
2 tbsp chocolate spread, such as Nutella
½ cup (150ml) buttermilk
1¼ cups (300ml) milk

TO SERVE
Chocolate sprinkles

MAKES
2½ cups (600ml)

A smoothie that's a real "spoil-yourself" treat as it hits the spot nicely when you've had a hard day and need cheering up. The slightly sour flavor of buttermilk balances the richness of the peanut butter and chocolate spread perfectly, and a good-sized ripe banana blended with the other ingredients will give you that all-important energy boost.

1 Peel the banana and cut it into chunks.

2 Place the banana in a juicer, add the peanut butter and chocolate spread and blend until smooth.

3 Pour in the buttermilk and milk and blend again until evenly mixed in.

4 Pour into glasses and scatter chocolate sprinkles over the top of each drink.

In the pink

INGREDIENTS

1 fresh peach or 2 canned peach halves in
fruit juice
6oz (175g) strawberries
¾ cup (175ml) cranberry juice
½ cup (150ml) coconut milk
1–2 tbsp maple syrup, or to taste

MAKES

3 cups (700ml)

Unsweetened coconut milk can be found amongst the Asian ingredients in supermarkets and oriental food stores but, if you prefer, you can make your own. To do this, grate the flesh of a fresh coconut into a cup measurement, tip into a bowl and pour in an equal amount of hot, rather than boiling, water, then leave the mix to stand for 30 minutes. Place a piece of muslin or a very fine sieve over another bowl and strain the coconut through it, pressing down on the pulp with a wooden spoon to extract as much liquid as you can. If the peach and strawberries are very ripe, the smoothie may be sweet enough to not need the maple syrup.

1 If using a fresh peach, peel it following the instructions on page 15, then quarter it and remove and discard the stone.

2 Hull the strawberries and cut any large fruits into halves or quarters.

3 Put the peach, strawberries, and cranberry juice in a juicer and blend until smooth. Add the coconut milk and maple syrup and blend again until combined.

4 Pour into glasses and serve with extra strawberries.

Liquid gold

All citrus fruits are rich in vitamin C, and oranges are no exception. They are also high in soluble fiber and pectin, which decrease the rate at which sugar is absorbed by the body. Florida's climate of hot sunshine followed by sudden cloudbursts of rain ensures the State's favorite fruit grows with a thinner peel and has more juice packed into it than oranges from other parts of the world.

1 If using fresh apricots, peel them following the instructions on page 15, then halve them and remove and discard the stones.

2 Peel the mango and cut the flesh away from the fibrous center stone with a sharp knife.

3 Peel the banana and cut it into chunks.

4 Put the apricots, mango, and banana in a juicer, add the orange juice and half the milk and blend until smooth. Add the rest of the milk and blend again until combined.

5 Pour into glasses and serve.

INGREDIENTS

2 fresh apricots or 4 canned apricot halves
   in fruit juice
1 medium mango
1 small banana
½ cup (150ml) orange juice
1¼ cups (300ml) milk

SERVES

3¾ cups (900ml)

Plums and custard smoothie

Best described as an indulgent dessert in a glass! Ideally, the custard needs to be of a pouring consistency, but if it is quite thick, simply increase the quantity of apple juice until the smoothie is the right consistency. You can use readymade custard for this, but if it isn't available, make your own—see below for a simple recipe.

1 Halve the plums and remove the stones. Place in a pan with the cinnamon, sugar, and 3 tablespoons water and simmer until the plums are soft. Leave to cool.

2 Tip the plums and their juices into a juicer, add the custard and blend until smooth.

3 Add the apple juice and blend again until combined.

4 Pour into glasses and serve at once.

To make your own custard:
Put 3 large egg yolks in a bowl and whisk in 1 tablespoon superfine sugar and 1 tablespoon cornflour. Heat a cup of milk until almost boiling, pour onto the egg yolk mixture, whisking constantly until combined. Pour the mixture back into the pan and stir over a low heat until the custard is thickened and smooth. Transfer to a bowl, press cling wrap over the surface of the custard to prevent a skin forming and leave to cool.

INGREDIENTS

14oz (400g) red plums
1 tsp ground cinnamon
2 tbsp superfine sugar
¾ cup (200ml) cold custard
½ cup (150ml) apple juice

MAKES

3¾ cups (900ml)

Prune and Earl Grey soother

Choose large, juicy prunes like the *pruneaux d'Agen* from southwest France to make this smoothie, but soak them first in the tea for 30 minutes to make them nice and plump. Earl Grey tea is milder than a strong breakfast tea and owes its distinctive flavor to oil extracted from the rind of the bergamot orange, an aromatic citrus fruit, which is added to the blend. It is named in honor of the 2nd Earl Grey, who was British Prime Minister in the 1830s and reputedly received a gift of tea flavored with bergamot that pleased him very much.

1 Put the prunes in a heatproof bowl and pour over the hot tea. Leave to stand for 30 minutes or until the tea is cold.

2 Peel the banana and cut it into chunks.

3 Cut the peel and pith away from the orange and divide it into segments.

4 Tip the prunes and tea into a juicer, add the banana and orange and blend until smooth.

5 Add the yogurt and milk and blend again until combined.

6 Pour into glasses over crushed ice and serve with a few pumpkin seeds sprinkled over each drink.

INGREDIENTS

10 pitted prunes
¾ cup (200ml) hot Earl Grey tea
1 banana
1 orange
½ cup (150ml) natural yogurt
¾ cup (200ml) milk

TO SERVE

Crushed ice
Pumpkin seeds

MAKES

3½ cups (800ml)

Rambutan, coconut, and kiwi cream

INGREDIENTS

8 rambutans
1 kiwi fruit
6oz (175g) wedge of honeydew melon
1tbsp fresh lime juice
½ cup (150ml) coconut water
1¼ cups (300ml) milk

MAKES

4¼ cups (1 litre)

Native to the Malay peninsula, rambutans are closely related to lychees, so if rambutans are not available this smoothie could be made using lychees instead. Rambutans differ from lychees in that they are slightly less acidic and their soft skins are covered in a bush of dense, red hairs. Grown throughout southeast Asia, their name derives from the Malay word "*rambut*", meaning hair, while the Vietnamese feel every day is a bad hair day for the hapless rambutan, dubbling it *chôm chôm* (messy hair).

1 Cut around each rambutan with a small sharp knife and peel away the skin. Halve the fruit inside and remove the stone, which can be stubbornly attached to the flesh.

2 Peel the kiwi fruit and cut the flesh into chunks. Peel the melon, discard the seeds and chop the flesh.

3 Put the rambutans, kiwi, melon, and lime juice in a juicer, add the coconut water and milk and blend until smooth.

4 Pour into glasses and serve with a stirrer or long spoon as the juice will separate if left to stand.

Raspberry cheesecake dream

Raspberries are thought to have originated in Asia but they are now grown in so many countries that they must be one of the world's favorite fruits. Most of us think of the berries as being deep, deep pink but, depending on where they are grown, raspberries come in a rainbow of colors including yellow, orange, and deep purple. Blitzing raspberries with cottage cheese to make this smoothie means you can enjoy one of your favorite desserts in a tall glass. For an even more authentic liquid cheesecake, sprinkle a layer of crushed oat biscuits over the top of each drink rather than adding extra raspberries.

1 Put the raspberries in a juicer, add the lime juice and blend until smooth. Push the purée through a sieve to remove the raspberry seeds, if preferred.

2 Return the raspberry purée to the rinsed-out juicer and add the milk, curd cheese, and honey. Blend until smooth.

3 Pour into glasses and serve topped with extra raspberries.

INGREDIENTS

6oz (175g) raspberries
Juice of 1 lime
1¼ cups (300ml) milk
3oz (75g) cottage cheese
2 tbsp honey

TO SERVE

Extra raspberries

MAKES

3 cups (700ml)

Rhubarb, pomegranate, and yogurt blast

This smoothie is best made when the new season's rhubarb has just arrived and the stalks are pink and tender rather than when they have become tougher, greener, and more acidic as the crop matures. An excellent source of vitamin C, rhubarb is also a good source of calcium, dietary fibre, and vitamin K, which is thought to help prevent diabetes. Used for thousands of years as a medicine by the Chinese to cure digestive problems, only the stalks are edible; the leaves contain dangerous toxins and must be cut off and discarded. Despite appearances, rhubarb is classified as a vegetable across most of the world, apart from the US where in 1947 a New York court deemed that it should be considered a fruit.

1 Cut the rhubarb stalks into short lengths. Peel, core, and roughly chop the apples.

2 Put the rhubarb and apples in a pan, add the orange juice and honey or sugar and simmer until the rhubarb is tender– about 6–8 minutes. Leave to cool.

3 Put the rhubarb mixture, including its juice, in a juicer, add the pomegranate juice and yogurt and blend until smooth.

4 Pour into glasses and serve.

INGREDIENTS

11oz (300g) rhubarb

2 apples

4 tbsp orange juice

2 tbsp honey or sugar, or to taste

1¼ cups (300ml) pomegranate juice

4 tbsp natural yogurt

MAKES

3¾ cups (900ml)

Sharon fruit, grapefruit, and orange smoothie

INGREDIENTS

2 sharon fruit

1 white grapefruit

Juice of 1 lemon

2 tbsp honey

1¼ cups (300ml) orange juice

2 tbsp natural yogurt

MAKES

2½ cups (600ml)

Round, red-gold sharon fruit may look like a quirky breed of heirloom tomato but these shiny-skinned fruit are in fact a berry which are native to Israel, where they are named after the country's Sharon Valley. Unripe sharon fruit are tannic and bitter but once fully ripe their flesh becomes soft and very sweet. Full of beta carotene, protein, and glucose, they're also a powerhouse of nutritional goodies.

1 Remove the stalks from the sharon fruit. Peel and cut the flesh into small pieces.

2 Cut the peel and pith away from the grapefruit and divide the flesh into segments.

3 Put the sharon fruit, grapefruit, lemon juice, and honey in a juicer, add the orange juice and blend until smooth.

4 Add the yogurt and blend again until evenly mixed. Pour into glasses and serve.

Strawberry and honey buttermilk smoothie

Honey is a useful sweetener for juices and smoothies as it adds its own mellow flavor and there are no stubborn granules of sugar that need to be dissolved. Honey is valued for its health-enhancing properties; to give us energy and build a strong immune system. The most highly-prized—and most expensive—honey is New Zealand's manuka honey, which is produced from the nectar the bees collect from manuka flowers that grow in the pollution-free East Cape region of the country. So full of natural sugars is manuka honey that it is a scientifically proven treatment for wounds, its density prevents bacteria from surviving once honey is spread over a wound.

1 Hull the strawberries and cut any larger fruits into halves or quarters.

2 Peel the banana and chop it into short lengths.

3 Put the strawberries and banana in a juicer, add the buttermilk, milk, and honey and blend until smooth.

4 Pour into glasses and serve.

INGREDIENTS

7oz (200g) strawberries
1 banana
1¼ cups (300ml) buttermilk
¾ cup (175ml) milk
1–2 tbsp honey, or to taste

MAKES

3 cups (700ml)

Tangerine dream

INGREDIENTS

2 tangerines

1 nectarine

4 medjool dates

1¾ cups (400ml) milk

½ cup (150ml) natural yogurt

TO SERVE

Wheatgerm

MAKES

3¾ cups (900ml)

Medjool dates have been called the "crown jewels of the date world" and these large fruit are truly something special. Like most dates they are dried, but with medjools their skin remains soft and inside there is plenty of sweet flesh sticking to the easy-to-remove long, thin pit. A good source of fiber with high levels of potassium, manganese, copper, and magnesium, medjool dates are high in fruit sugar too, each date containing around 55 calories. Some dates are treated with sulphur to preserve their color, but they are also available unsulphured.

1 Peel the tangerines and pull away all the loose pith. Divide the fruit into segments. Halve the nectarine, remove the stone and chop the flesh into chunks.

2 Stone the dates and chop coarsely.

3 Put the tangerines, nectarine, and dates in a juicer, add the milk and blend for about 1 minute until smooth. Strain, if preferred, to remove any residual pith from the tangerine or flecks of nectarine skin. Return to the juicer, add the yogurt and blend again.

4 Pour into glasses, sprinkle a little wheatgerm on top of each drink and serve.

Strawberry and coconut blush

Coconut water is the clear, sweet juice drained from a young, green coconut and is one of the most refreshing drinks there is. It also contains a unique mix of nutrients, including high levels of bone-strengthening calcium, amino acids that are the building blocks of proteins in our bodies, and enzymes to aid digestion. The electrolytes, potassium and sodium, are two other vital nutrients in coconut water, as these replenish hydration levels when fluids in the body are depleted through over-strenuous exercise or stomach complaints like diarrhoea or dysentery.

1 Hull the strawberries and cut any large fruits into halves or quarters.

2 Twist the stalk off the pear, cut it into quarters, remove the core and peel.

3 Put the strawberries and pear in a juicer, add the coconut water and pineapple juice and blend until smooth.

4 Strain or skin off any froth, if preferred, and pour into glasses. Serve with a few freeze-dried strawberries sprinkled over each drink. If not serving straight away the drink will separate, so stir it up before drinking using a fork or a balloon whisk.

INGREDIENTS
6oz (175g) strawberries
1 pear
½ cup (150ml) coconut water
¾ cup (200ml) pineapple juice

TO SERVE
Freeze-dried strawberries

MAKES
2½ cups (600ml)

Papaya, clementine, and peach smoothie

INGREDIENTS

1 yellow-fleshed peach

½ medium papaya, weighing about 6oz (175g)

2 clementines

1¼ cups (300ml) apple juice

½ cup (150ml) natural yogurt

MAKES

3¾ cups (900ml)

As papayas vary so much in size I've provided an approximate weight to give you an idea of what I think a papaya classed as "medium" should weigh, but take this as a guide; if you use a larger fruit, add extra apple juice or water if the smoothie seems too thick. Known as paw paws in the West Indian islands, Central America, and Australia, papayas can be small and pear-shaped with yellow-orange skins or as big as vegetable marrows with deep green skins. Their many health benefits are well documented and include boosting the immune system, helping to prevent colds and flu, and alleviating the side effects of cancer treatments. Used externally, papaya peel can also be used to treat skin wounds that are slow to heal.

1 Peel the peach following the instructions on page 15, then cut it in half, remove the stone and slice or chop the flesh.

2 Scoop the seeds out of the papaya, cut away the skin and chop the flesh into chunks.

3 Peel the clementines, pulling away any loose strands of white pith.

4 Put the peach, papaya, and clementines in a juicer, add the apple juice and yogurt and blend until smooth.

5 Strain to remove any remaining pith from the clementines, pour into glasses and serve.

Shakes

Shakes

Not just shakes, but slushies, crushes, floats, and ice pops too. This chapter is all about having fun with the family by making creamy milkshakes and frozen drinks to cool you all down on a summer's day.

Ice pops are likely to be the most popular with kids and there are a few tips that are useful for making these. When pouring the juice into the lolly molds, remember that as the liquid freezes it expands, so avoid filling the molds right to the top, especially if they have clip-on lids. Once the molds have been filled, put them in the freezer until the juice is still soft enough for popsicle sticks to be pushed in but sufficiently frozen to hold the sticks in place and stop them floating to the surface.

Fruits become less sweet and their flavor less pronounced when frozen, so although you might not sweeten a juice, you may find a frozen slushie or ice pop needs a little sugar, maple syrup, or honey added to bring out the flavor of the fruit.

When un-molding frozen ice pops, if they stick stubbornly and won't budge, warm the molds with your hands or a warm cloth or dip them very briefly in hot water to loosen them sufficiently to be lifted out. Avoid tugging on the sticks to remove them as the stick could snap.

Banoffee beauty

INGREDIENTS

1 banana

2 tbsp dulce de leche

½ cup (150ml) natural yogurt

1 cup (225ml) milk

*4 scoops of banana ice cream, or use
    vanilla if banana is not available*

4 amaretti biscuits, crushed

MAKES

3½ cups (800ml)

Dulce de leche is sweetened milk that has been cooked until it becomes thick, golden, and sticky like molten English-style toffee and in Brazil, Argentina, and Uruguay it is practically the national dish. Young and old spread it on bread, add it to desserts, ice creams, and cakes and drizzle it liberally over pancakes. Here I've used it to make a wickedly delicious shake.

1 Peel the banana and cut it into chunks.

2 Put the banana in a juicer, add the dulce de leche, yogurt, and milk and blend until smooth.

3 Add the ice cream and blend again briefly until combined.

4 Pour into glasses and serve at once with the crushed amaretti sprinkled over each drink.

Totally tropical shake

INGREDIENTS

½ medium papaya

1 banana

½ cup (150ml) milk

½ cup (150ml) coconut water

2 tsp lime juice

2 scoops of vanilla ice cream

2 scoops of mango sorbet

MAKES

3¾ cups (900ml)

Lots of favorite exotic flavors like mango, coconut, vanilla, and papaya come together in this delicious shake—you'll be imagining yourself stretched out on a white coral beach with the Caribbean gently lapping around your toes. Choose a good-quality vanilla ice cream, preferably one with the seeds from vanilla pods mixed into it, as it will have a better flavor and will make the shake beautifully creamy.

1 Scoop the seeds out of the papaya and peel away the skin.

2 Peel the banana and cut it into chunks.

3 Put the papaya and banana into a juicer, add the milk, coconut water, and lime juice and blend until smooth.

4 Add the vanilla ice cream and mango sorbet and blend again until combined. Pour into glasses and serve at once.

Berry and grape shake

The wonderfully rich color of this shake will make you want to drink it as soon as you've poured it into a glass. Grape juice provides a lot of natural energy, so not only is the drink refreshing and satisfying, it's energizing too, helping to keep you going the whole day long.

1 Hull the strawberries and halve or quarter any large fruits.

2 Put the strawberries in a juicer, add the grape juice and honey and blend until smooth.

3 Add the frozen raspberry yogurt and blend again until combined.

4 Pour into glasses and serve at once.

INGREDIENTS

4oz (115g) strawberries
1¼ cups (300ml) red grape juice
2 tsp honey
6 scoops of frozen raspberry yogurt

MAKES

3 cups (700ml)

Chilled caffé latte shake

Make up your coffee for this shake using ground coffee beans in a filter or an Italian coffee machine rather than instant coffee granules, as the brew needs to be strong to give the drink plenty of warm, Italian flavor. Add a cloud of whipping cream piped in a swirl on top and a sprinkle of ground cinnamon, close your eyes and you'll be transported back to that little café in your favorite Florentine or Roman square.

1 Put the coffee, milk, and ice cream in a juicer and blend until smooth.

2 Put a couple of tablespoons of crushed ice in each glass—tall ones with a handle work best—pour in the contents of the juicer and top with spiral of whipping cream.

3 Sprinkle a little ground cinnamon over the cream and serve at once with straws and long spoons.

INGREDIENTS
1½ cups (350ml) strong black coffee, chilled
¾ cup (175ml) milk
6 scoops of coffee ice cream

TO SERVE
Crushed ice
Whipped cream
Ground cinnamon

MAKES
2½ cups (600ml)

Carrot, physalis, and mango slushy

INGREDIENTS

1 medium mango
6 physalis
½ cup (150ml) orange juice
½ cup (115ml) carrot juice
2 tbsp superfine sugar

TO SERVE

Edible gold sprinkles
Extra whole physalis

MAKES

6

Physalis, also known as the Cape gooseberry, must be one of the prettiest of fruits, with shiny golden berries hidden under lacy Chinese lantern hoods. Unfortunately, these fruits are rather a case of style over substance; they look gorgeous but they can be disappointing to eat on their own, as they lack any distinctive flavor. Added to a juice, however, physalis work well and when left in their gossamer-thin wrappers they make the perfect decoration for any drink.

1 Peel the mango and cut the flesh away from the fibrous center stone. Slice or chop the flesh.

2 Remove the physalis from their papery cases.

3 Put the mango flesh, physalis, orange juice, carrot juice, and sugar in a juicer and blend until smooth.

4 Pour into a plastic freezer container and freeze for about 2 hours or until the mixture is frozen around the edges but still soft in the middle. Break up the frozen parts with a fork and mix with the soft center. Freeze again for 1 hour.

5 Fork up the mixture and spoon it into glasses or dishes. Serve dusted with edible gold sprinkles and extra physalis with their cases peeled back but still attached to the fruit.

Choc 'n' apricot pops

Fromage frais is a creamy, soft cheese made from whole or skim milk and cream. Also known as fromage blanc, it was originally from northern France and southern Belgium but is now widely available both flavored with different fruits or in its natural state. Eaten on its own, fromage frais has a fairly tart flavor and as fruit tends to become less sweet when frozen, apricot jam or honey is added to the mixture to make the ice pops more appealing to junior —and adult—taste buds.

1 If using fresh apricots, if you wish, then halve them and remove the stones.

2 Put the apricot halves in a juicer, add the fromage frais and apricot jam and blend until smooth.

3 Spoon into lolly moulds and freeze until almost firm. Push a stick into each ice pop and freeze again until solid.

4 Chop or break the chocolate into small pieces and place in a heatproof bowl over a pan of simmering water. Leave until the chocolate has melted, stirring until smooth. Remove the bowl from the pan and leave until the chocolate is cool but still liquid.

5 Spread out the chopped hazelnuts on a plate. Unmould the ice pops and dip the tops of them first in the melted chocolate and then in the hazelnuts. Place on a foil-lined plate and freeze again briefly until the chocolate has set.

INGREDIENTS

6 fresh apricots or 12 apricot halves,
* canned in fruit juice*
6oz (175g) natural fromage frais
2 tbsp apricot jam or honey
3oz (75g) dark chocolate
2oz (50g) chopped toasted hazelnuts

MAKES

6 (using ¼ cup /50ml molds)

Chocolate, hazelnut, and vanilla velvet

What can I say about a blitz of chocolate, milk, yogurt and the very best vanilla ice cream that won't have you rushing to the juicer to prepare a long, cool glass of this dreamy drink? Nothing, I hope, because it's totally, utterly irresistible and if you don't believe me, just try it for yourself.

1 Put the chocolate and hazelnut spread in a juicer.

2 Add the milk and yogurt and blend until smooth. Add the ice cream and blend again until combined but the ice cream hasn't completely melted.

3 Pour into glasses and serve sprinkled with chopped toasted hazelnuts and mini marshmallows.

INGREDIENTS
4oz (115g) chocolate and hazelnut spread, such as Nutella
1¼ cups (300ml) milk
4 tbsp natural yogurt
4 scoops of vanilla ice cream

TO SERVE
Chopped toasted hazelnuts and mini marshmallows

MAKES
3 cups (700ml)

Ice pop flares

INGREDIENTS

½ cup (150ml) cranberry and juice
½ cup (150ml) red grape juice
½ cup (150ml) orange juice
½ cup (150ml) apple juice

MAKES

8 (using ¼ cup /75ml lolly molds)

These lollies can be made with any combination of juices, but go for contrasting colors in the two layers for maximum dramatic effect. If you make your own fruit juices, you could use mango juice instead of orange and strawberry, or raspberry instead of cranberry.

1 Mix the cranberry and red grape juices together in a jug and pour into the molds so they are half full.

2 Freeze for about 1 hour or until the juices are almost solid. Push in the lolly sticks.

3 Mix the orange and apple juices together and use to top up the molds.

4 Return the lollies to the freezer for 3–4 hours or until completely solid before removing them from the molds.

Banana, mango, and yogurt ice pops

The best way to describe these ice pops is as "smoothies on a stick", and they are just the thing to cool you down on a hot day. For a richer flavor, all or part of the yogurt can be replaced with heavy cream.

1 Peel the banana and cut it into chunks.

2 Peel the mango and cut the flesh away from the fibrous center stone.

3 Put the banana and mango in a juicer, add the yogurt, orange juice, lime juice, and honey and blend until smooth.

4 Pour into the molds and freeze until almost firm. Push in the lolly sticks and freeze again until solid.

INGREDIENTS

1 banana

1 medium mango

1 cup (225ml) natural or coconut-flavored
  Greek yogurt

¾ cup (175ml) orange juice

1 tbsp lime juice

2 tbsp honey

MAKES

8 (using ¼ cup /75ml lolly molds)

Iced citrus tea

If you're a tea drinker, this refreshing brew is just what you need to cool you down on a hot summer's day. Green tea imparts a subtle, mild tea flavor, so if you prefer something stronger, substitute a black tea such as Assam or Darjeeling. As green tea is lighter than black tea, boil the water and then leave it for about 1 minute before pouring it over the tea bags so it doesn't scald the delicate leaves and spoil their flavor. Alternatively, mint or a herbal tea could be used.

1 Squeeze the juice from the lemon and the orange into a measuring jug—you will need about ½ cup of the combined juices, so top up with extra lemon or orange juice, if necessary.

2 Put the tea bags in a heatproof jug and pour over the boiling water. Set aside to brew for 5–10 minutes, depending on how strong you like your tea. Remove the tea bags and leave to cool completely.

3 Put the tea and citrus juices in a juicer, add the lemon sorbet and blend until smooth. Taste the tea and sweeten with a little honey or sugar, if desired.

4 Pour into cups or glasses over crushed ice and serve at once topped with small orange wedges.

MERINGUES

1 lemon
1 orange
4 green tea bags
2½ cups (600ml) water that has been boiled and left to stand for 1 minute
4 scoops of lemon sorbet
Honey or sugar, to taste

TO SERVE
Crushed ice and small orange wedges

MAKES
3¼ cups (800ml)

Peach, banana, and maple shake

We have the maple tree to thank for the sweet sap that oozes from its trunk, ready to be boiled down to produce the wonderfully toffee-flavored syrup that tastes so good poured over everything from pancakes to ice cream or used to sweeten a drink. During the winter in cold climates such as Canada, the largest producer of maple syrup, the trees store starch in their roots and trunks that acts as anti freeze and which converts into sugar when the sap rises in spring. The sap is then drained off through pipes inserted into holes in the trunks and carried to sugar shacks, the boiling houses where the syrup is produced. Packed with antioxidants and minerals such as manganese for strong muscles and zinc to help build white blood cells, maple syrup is much more than just sugar by another name.

1 Peel the peach, following the instructions on page 15, then halve it, remove the stone and chop the flesh.

2 Peel the banana and cut it into chunks.

3 Put the peach, banana, milk, and maple syrup into a juicer and blend until smooth.

4 Add the ice cream and blend again until combined. Pour into glasses and serve at once.

INGREDIENTS

1 white-fleshed peach
1 banana
1¼ cups (300ml) milk
2 tbsp maple syrup
4 scoops of vanilla ice cream

MAKES

3 cups (700ml)

Coconut, chocolate, and banana shake

Coconut milk adds extra creaminess to this rich and indulgent shake, making it a special treat for children and grownups alike. For an extra chocolate high, blend a couple of tablespoonfuls of chocolate spread with the other ingredients—and enjoy!

1 Peel the banana and cut it into chunks.

2 Place the banana in a juicer, add the milk and coconut milk and blend until smooth.

3 Add the ice cream and blend again briefly so the mixture is smooth but the ice cream has not completely melted.

4 Pour into glasses and serve at once sprinkled with chocolate sugar strands.

INGREDIENTS

1 banana
1¼ cup (300ml) milk
½ cup (115ml) coconut milk
4 scoops of chocolate ice cream

TO SERVE

Chocolate vermicelli

MAKES

3¾ cups (800ml)

Kiwi, peach, and orange confetti crush

INGREDIENTS

1¼ cups (350ml) orange juice
½ cup (150ml) apple juice
1 large orange
1 peach
1 kiwi fruit

TO SERVE

Sugar sprinkles

MAKES

6

If your children are reluctant to eat their fruit and vegetables, turning the unpopular produce into an eye-catching bowl of frozen loveliness is bound to tempt even the most reluctant junior appetite. This crush can be made with virtually any combination of fruits and juices but, depending on what you use, you may need to sweeten the mix with a little honey if it's too sharp.

1 Pour the orange and apple juices into a freezer container and freeze until not quite solid.

2 Cut the peel and pith away from the orange and divide the flesh into segments, discarding any pips.

3 Peel the peach following the instructions on page 15, halve, remove the stone and cut into chunks.

4 Peel the kiwi fruit and cut into chunks.

5 Break up the frozen juice with a fork into chunks that will fit inside a juicer, add the orange, peach, and kiwi fruit and blitz until the juice is crushed and the fruit is chopped into small pieces.

6 Spoon into glasses or dishes, add a scattering of sugar sprinkles and serve at once.

Mango coolie

A shake that can be made with any number of different fruits from peaches and strawberries to apricots, cherries, and papayas, just team your chosen fruit with a similar colored sorbet or ice cream.

INGREDIENTS

1 large mango
1¼ cups (300ml) buttermilk
2 tsp maple syrup
4 scoops of mango sorbet

MAKES

3 cups (700ml)

1 Peel the mango and cut the flesh away from the fibrous center stone.

2 Put the mango flesh in a juicer, add the buttermilk and maple syrup and blend until smooth.

3 Add the mango sorbet and blend again until combined. Pour into glasses and serve at once.

Plum, strawberry, and cherry chiller

Plums can be small, round, and sunshine yellow, oval with mottled red-gold skins, or plump and every shade of red from scarlet to a dark, almost black, claret. Choose ripe plums for this recipe, with deep red skins and plenty of juicy, sweet flesh; if the plums are under-ripe, their stones will be difficult to remove and the flesh tart, meaning more sugar will be needed to sweeten the mix.

1 Halve the plums and remove the stones. Hull the strawberries.

2 Pull the stalks from the cherries, halve and pick out the pits with your fingers or use a cherry pitting tool.

3 Cut the plums and strawberries into even-size pieces and spread out on a baking sheet lined with cling wrap with the cherries. Sprinkle with the sugar and freeze until firm.

4 Break up the fruit into pieces that will fit into a juicer goblet, and blend in batches with the apple juice until combined but the fruit is not quite reduced to a purée.

5 Spoon into dishes or glasses and serve at once.

INGREDIENTS

4 red plums
5oz (150g) strawberries
4oz (115g) red cherries
2 tbsp superfine sugar
2½ cups (600ml) apple juice

MAKES

6–8

Mango and lime lollies

Sprinkling these lollies with pink crystal sugar turns them
into the perfect treat for a girlie get-together, such as a
bachelorette party or a baby shower. Blending coconut
cream and heavy cream with the mango makes these
a real indulgence, but for a less calorific alternative,
substitute the coconut cream with coconut water and the
heavy cream with natural yogurt.

1 Peel the mango and cut the flesh away from the fibrous
center stone.

2 Put the mango flesh in a juicer and add the lime juice, honey,
and coconut cream. Blend until smooth and transfer to a bowl.

3 Whip the cream until just holding its shape and fold into the
mango purée.

4 Spoon into lolly molds and freeze until almost firm. Push in
lolly sticks and freeze again until solid.

5 Remove the lollies from their molds and allow the outsides
to soften for just long enough for the sugar to stick to them.
Sprinkle over the pink crystal sugar and immediately lay
the lollies on a plate lined with cling wrap and freeze again
until solid.

INGREDIENTS

1 medium mango
Juice of 1 lime
1 tbsp clear honey
4 tbsp coconut cream
½ cup (150ml) double cream
Pink crystal sugar

MAKES

6 (using ¼ cup /75ml lolly molds)

Key lime shake

INGREDIENTS

4 key limes or 2 ordinary limes

2 tbsp superfine sugar

1¼ cups (300ml) milk

4 scoops of vanilla ice cream

MAKES

2½ cups (600ml)

Key limes take their name from their association with the Florida Keys and the classic dessert, key lime pie. Smaller than other limes, measuring only 1–2in in diameter, the limes also have thinner skins, a stronger aroma, and a sharper flavor so, if you use them for this shake, you may need to increase the amount of sugar you add so that it is not too tart.

1 Cut up the limes into small pieces and put them in a juicer with the sugar and milk.

2 Blend thoroughly until only tiny flecks of lime zest can be seen. Strain through a fine sieve, pressing the pulp with the back of a wooden spoon to extract all the liquid from it.

3 Return the strained lime milk to the juicer, add the ice cream and a few drops of green food coloring, if you want the shake to have a more pronounced green color, and blend again until just combined.

4 Pour into glasses and serve at once.

Strawberry yogurt swirls

Instead of strawberries, these jolly ice lollies could be made with raspberries, blueberries, or blackberries, but if you decide on raspberries or blackberries, after you've blitzed them with the orange juice you'll need to sieve the purée to remove the seeds or the lollies will have pips in them and younger members of the family are sure to complain—the older ones might as well!

1 Hull the strawberries and halve or quarter any large fruits.

2 Put the strawberries in a juicer and add the orange juice. Blend to a purée.

3 Put half the strawberry purée in a bowl and stir in the yogurt and honey.

4 Fill the lolly molds with alternate spoonfuls of the purée and the yogurt and swirl the mixtures together using a cocktail stick.

5 Freeze until just firm, push a lolly stick into each mold and freeze again until solid.

INGREDIENTS

7oz (200g) strawberries
4 tbsp orange juice
¾ cup (200ml) natural yogurt
2 tsp clear honey

MAKES

4 (using ½ cup /115ml lolly molds)

Raspberry and banana lollies

Whole milk, semi-skim or skim milk can be used to make these lollies, although the higher the fat content of the milk the creamier the lollies will be. They could be made with strawberries instead of raspberries, if you prefer, in which case there is no need to sieve the purée.

1 Put the raspberries in a juicer, add 3 tablespoons of the milk and blend to a purée. Push through a sieve to remove the raspberry seeds.

2 Peel the banana and cut it into chunks.

3 Return the sieved raspberry purée to the rinsed-out juicer and add the banana and the rest of the milk. Blend until smooth.

4 Pour into the lolly molds and freeze until almost firm. Push a stick into each mold and freeze again until solid.

INGREDIENTS
7oz (200g) raspberries
¾ cup (200ml) milk
1 small banana
2 tbsp honey

MAKES
6 (using ¼ cup /65ml lolly molds)

Pineapple and apricot slushy

INGREDIENTS

1 small pineapple

3 whole fresh apricots, or 6 halves
  canned in fruit juice

1 banana

1¼ cups (300ml) orange juice

2 tbsp dried milk powder

2 tbsp superfine sugar

MAKES
6

When making drinks, a can of skim milk powder is a useful store-cupboard standby as it can be added to the other ingredients without needing to be reconstituted first, giving the finished drink—or in this case, slushy—a creamier consistency. Skim milk powder is virtually fat free but all the protein, calcium, and vitamins found in whole milk are retained during the skimming process.

1 Cut the top off the pineapple, peel and remove the brown "eyes" and the tough center core and chop the flesh into small chunks.

2 If using fresh apricots, peel them following the instructions on page 15, then halve them and remove the stones.

3 Peel the banana and cut it into chunks.

4 Put the pineapple chunks, apricot halves, and the banana in a juicer. Add the orange juice, milk powder, and sugar and blend until smooth.

5 Pour into a plastic freezer container and freeze for about 2 hours or until the mix is frozen around the edges. Mash up the frozen part with a fork, mixing it with the softer mixture in the middle. Return to the freezer for another hour and break up again with the fork.

6 Spoon the slushy into glasses or dishes and serve at once topped with pineapple and apricot slices.

Raspberry, kiwi, and orange crush

INGREDIENTS

2 kiwi fruit
1¼ cups (300ml) orange juice
4 scoops of raspberry sorbet

TO SERVE

Fresh raspberries

MAKES

3 cups (700ml)

Plenty of legends have grown up as to who invented sorbets, one theory cites Marco Polo with bringing frozen fruit desserts back with him from China. Another, maybe not as crazy as it sounds bearing in mind the Roman Emperor involved, credits Nero as the sorbet's creator, when he employed relays of runners along the Appian way to carry buckets of snow to his banqueting hall in the mountains where it was mixed with honey and wine. Yet another theory says it was Catherine de'Medici who took frozen desserts with her from Italy to France when she married King Henry II. In Victorian England, a sorbet always contained alcohol and tended to resemble a frozen rum punch or claret cup, but today it has come to mean a low-cal fruit ice, similar to a 'sherbert' but with no dairy products added. Here the sorbet makes a refreshing drink.

1 Peel the kiwi fruit and cut them into chunks or slices.

2 Place the kiwi in a juicer and add the orange juice and raspberry sorbet. Blend until smooth.

3 Pour into glasses and serve with fresh raspberries.

Strawberry, peach, and coconut slush

INGREDIENTS

2 peaches

2 bananas

2 tbsp brown sugar

7oz (200g) strawberries

½ cup (150ml) pineapple juice

½ cup (150ml) coconut milk

4 tbsp crushed ice

SERVES

6

This is a lovely dessert for a sunny day and much more interesting than plain ice cream. Nectarines or apricots can be used instead of peaches and raspberries, or kiwi fruit instead of the strawberries.

1 Peel the peaches if you wish, then cut them in half and remove the stones. Chop the flesh into small chunks.

2 Peel the bananas and cut them into thick slices.

3 Spread out the peaches and bananas on a tray lined with cling wrap, sprinkle over the sugar and stir to coat the fruit. Freeze until solid.

4 Hull the strawberries, quarter or halve any large fruits and put them in a juicer. Add the pineapple juice and coconut milk and blend until smooth.

5 Break up the peaches and bananas into pieces small enough to fit in the juicer goblet and add half the crushed ice. Blend for 5 seconds then add the rest of the ice and blend until slushy.

6 Spoon into glasses or dishes and serve at once.

Strawberry and chocolate shake

A combination of flavors that will prove very popular with children as not only are strawberries and chocolate likely to be two of their favorite things, they also combine brilliantly to make a colorful shake.

1 Hull the strawberries and cut larger fruits into halves or quarters.

2 Put the strawberries in a juicer, add the milk and blend until smooth.

3 Add the chocolate ice cream and blend again until combined.

4 Pour into glasses and serve with extra strawberries.

INGREDIENTS

6oz (175g) strawberries
1¼ cups (300ml) milk
4 scoops of chocolate ice cream

TO SERVE

Extra fresh strawberries

MAKES

3 cups (700ml)

Raspberry and banana cola float

Instead of cola, you could make this shake with sparkling lemonade or bitter lemon, ginger ale, or sparkling orange drink, but cola does add its own unique flavor to the fruit and ice cream. Raspberries add a vibrant red hue but you can ring the changes by substituting the same quantity of other fruits such as mangoes, peaches, or cherries.

1 Put the raspberries in a juicer, add 2 tablespoons of the orange juice and blend to a purée. Sieve the purée to remove the pips.

2 Rinse out the juicer and return the raspberry purée to it. Peel the banana, chop it into chunks and add with the rest of the orange juice. Blend again until smooth.

3 Put a scoop of ice cream in 4 tall glasses and pour in the raspberry and banana purée.

4 Top up with the cola and serve at once with long spoons to stir up the shakes and scoop every last drop from the bottom of the glasses.

INGREDIENTS

8oz (225g) raspberries
½ cup (150ml) orange juice
1 banana
330ml can cola
4 scoops of vanilla ice cream

TO SERVE

Redcurrant sprigs

MAKES

4 drinks

Strawberry and redcurrant delight

INGREDIENTS

5oz (150g) redcurrants
6oz (175g) strawberries
½ cup (150ml) white grape juice
2½ cups (600ml) sparkling mineral water

MAKES

3 cups (750ml) before the sparkling
mineral water, if added

Look for cartons of white grape juice that haven't been sweetened as the natural sweetness of 100% juice and the strawberries provide the perfect balance in this drink. Reputed to cure migraines if drunk neat first thing in the morning, white grape juice also replenishes stocks of iron in the body and fights tiredness if you're having a stressful day. As it is so easy to digest, recent medical research points to it being a suitable first juice to introduce into the diet of toddlers and babies over six months old.

1 Strip the redcurrants from their stalks and place in a juicer.

2 Hull the strawberries and halve or quarter any large fruits.

3 Add the strawberries to the juicer with the white grape juice and blend until smooth.

4 Divide the strawberry purée between the glasses and top up with the mineral water. Serve as soon as the excess bubbles settle down.

Orange and buttermilk shake

Chia seeds are one of the newer superfoods to dazzle us with their health-giving properties and it's true that these unassuming tiny black and white seeds do punch above their weight when it comes to doing us good. One of the best sources of plant-based protein, the seeds are packed with omega 3s, the essential fatty acids that promise us Olympic-grade muscles, super-smooth skin, and a healthy heart. Part of the mint family, chia seeds were a staple food of the Aztecs and if you consider those Amazonian tribes often ran for days fortified with nothing more than a handful of chia seeds wrapped in a leaf, their reputation as a superfood looks pretty impressive.

1 Put the orange juice, buttermilk, maple syrup, and chia seeds in a juicer and blend until combined.

2 Add the orange sorbet and blend again until smooth and frothy.

3 Pour into glasses and sprinkle with extra chia seeds before serving.

INGREDIENTS
½ cup (115ml) orange juice
1 cup (225ml) buttermilk
2 tsp maple syrup
2 tbsp chia seeds
6 scoops of orange sorbet

TO SERVE
Extra chia seeds

MAKES
2½ cups (600ml)

Tiramisu heaven

Everyone's favorite Italian dessert is transformed in this recipe into a silky glass of paradise. If you're making the shake for grownups, a good slug of a coffee liqueur such as Tia Maria or Kahlua will guarantee the party goes with a swing, so be sure to make plenty!

1 Dissolve the coffee granules in 1 tablespoon boiling water, stir until smooth and set aside to cool.

2 Put the ice cream and mascarpone in a juicer, add the dissolved coffee and crumble in the sponge finger. Blend until smooth.

3 Pour into glasses and serve with extra sponge fingers for dunking. Dust the top of each drink with a little cocoa powder.

INGREDIENTS

1 tbsp instant coffee granules
4 scoops of vanilla ice cream
½ cup (150ml) milk
6oz (175g) mascarpone
1 sponge finger

TO SERVE

Extra sponge fingers and cocoa powder

MAKES

2 cups (500ml)

Strawberry, almond, and apple float

INGREDIENTS
1 apple
5oz (150g) strawberries
½ cup (150ml) apple juice
2 tbsp ground almonds
8 small scoops of frozen strawberry yogurt

MAKES
2½ cups (600ml)

Ground almonds add texture as well as flavor to this shake which is tangy rather than very creamy as the strawberries, apple juice, and almonds are blitzed with frozen strawberry yogurt rather than ice cream. If you prefer to use ice cream, that's fine, as the shake will taste equally delicious.

1 Peel, core, and chop the apple.

2 Hull the strawberries and halve or quarter any large fruits.

3 Put the apple, strawberries, and apple juice in a juicer and blend until smooth. Add the ground almonds and 4 scoops of the frozen strawberry yogurt and blend again.

4 Pour into glasses and serve with the remaining scoops of ice cream floated on top of the drinks.

Summer berry zing

This frozen combination of fresh berries is a real taste of summer, and when the fruits are in season they should be sweet enough blended with the raspberry sorbet not to need extra sugar. However, if the mix is a little sharp for your taste, add a little honey or superfine sugar.

1 Hull the strawberries and halve or quarter any large fruits.

2 Put the strawberries, raspberries, blueberries, and blackberries in a juicer, add the orange juice and raspberry sorbet and blend until just combined.

3 Spoon into glasses or dishes and serve at once.

INGREDIENTS

6oz (175g) strawberries
5oz (150g) raspberries
5oz (150g) blueberries
4oz (115g) blackberries
1¼ cups (300ml) orange juice
6 scoops of raspberry sorbet

MAKES

6

Watermelon and pink grapefruit slushy

One of the largest members of the citrus family, grapefruit can be white, pink, or red-fleshed. The redder the fruit, the higher concentration of vitamins and minerals it contains, plus it has increased levels of lycopene, the natural antioxidant—also found in watermelon—that helps the body fight free radicals which can lead to heart disease and cancer. Grapefruit also cleanses the digestive system, detoxes the liver, and helps reduce blood cholesterol, so it works hard for its place in the fruit bowl.

1 Peel the skin off the watermelon and pick out any seeds. Cut the flesh into chunks.

2 Hull the strawberries and halve or quarter any large fruits.

3 Put the watermelon, strawberries, grapefruit juice, and honey into a juicer and blend until smooth.

4 Pour into a plastic freezer container and freeze for about 2 hours or until the mixture is frozen around the edges but still soft in the center. Break up the frozen parts with a fork and mix with the softer center. Freeze again for 1 hour.

5 Fork up the mixture and spoon into glasses or dishes. Serve with watermelon wedges.

INGREDIENTS
1½lb (700g) wedge of watermelon
5oz (150g) strawberries
¾ cup (200ml) pink grapefruit juice
2 tbsp honey

TO SERVE
Watermelon wedges

MAKES
6

Juices

Juices

Few things can beat a freshly made juice that you've prepared yourself, and the minute you pour it into a long, cool glass you just know it's going to make you feel good.

Fresh juices are highly nutritious and are an excellent way of helping fussy children—and adults—who normally fall short of their "five-a-day," to up their intake of fresh fruit and vegetables. Around 95% of the nutrients in fruit and vegetables are contained in their juice and the big advantage that homemade juices have over bought ones is that you decide exactly what goes into them. If you prefer something tangy you can squeeze in some fresh lemon or lime juice to sharpen the flavor or, if you have a sweet tooth, rather than just add sugar, you can drizzle in maple syrup, honey, or even a flavored syrup like grenadine, strawberry, or chocolate.

Not only are juices quick and easy to make, they're fresh and tasty and full of valuable nutrients too. You can enjoy them throughout the day and when you're short of time and need an instant pick-me-up, they're the ultimate fast food.

Apple, mint, and lemon grass sparkler

Native to India and tropical Asia, lemon grass is also known as citronella and is an essential ingredient in Thai cuisine, while in south India it is infused to make a herbal tea. The gray-green stems resemble the root end of spring onions, but there the similarity ends as lemon grass stalks are made up of tightly packed woody layers that impart a sweet lemony aroma and flavor. Most of the flavor of lemon grass is in the bulb end of the stalks, which should feel firm and heavy and have no bruising or other marks. If the stalks feel light they will probably have dried out too much and will lack the intensity of flavor of fresh lemon grass.

INGREDIENTS

1 apple

4 sprigs of fresh mint

½ lemon grass stalk, split lengthways, any tough outer leaves removed and the stalk finely chopped

½ cup (150ml) apple juice

1½ cups (350ml) ginger ale

TO SERVE

Apple slices and fresh mint sprigs,

MAKES

2½ cups (600ml)

1 Cut the apple into quarters, remove the core and peel the skin.

2 Put the apple in a juicer, add the mint and lemon grass and pour in the apple juice. Blend thoroughly so the lemon grass is pulverized and the mixture is smooth.

3 Strain into a jug and pour in the ginger ale, stirring to mix everything together.

4 Pour into glasses and serve with apple slices and fresh mint sprigs in each glass.

Blackberry, apple, and mint haze

Blackberry, apple, and mint is a classic flavor combination that works equally well in a juice as in a homely fruit pie. Blackberries are high in antioxidants but contain numerous tiny seeds that you may prefer to strain out. On the nutritional side, the seeds are rich in omega 3 and linoleic acid, so if you can bear to leave them in you'll have an extra healthy boost.

1 Cut the rind off the melon, scoop out the seeds and chop the flesh into chunks.

2 Put the melon and blackberries in a juicer, add the apple juice and mint and blend until smooth.

3 Push through a sieve to remove the blackberry seeds, if preferred, pour into glasses and serve decorated with small sprigs of mint. The juice can also be served as a long drink topped up with still or sparkling mineral water.

INGREDIENTS
7oz (200g) wedge of Ogen or Galia melon
6oz (175g) blackberries
1¼ cups (300ml) apple juice
1 tbsp roughly chopped fresh mint

TO SERVE
Mint sprigs

MAKES
2 cups (500ml)

Carrot, pear, and apricot juice

INGREDIENTS

6 apricot halves, fresh or canned in fruit
  juice
1 ripe but firm pear
1½ cups (350ml) carrot juice

MAKES

2½ cups (600ml)

Popular with all ages and endlessly versatile whether eaten raw with dips, added to a cake, or puréed for a soup, the dependable carrot regularly finds its way into most people's shopping baskets. As a ready-made juice it is excellent and while it can be blended with all sorts of fruits to make mixed drinks, carrot juice is also sufficiently refreshing to drink on its own—about the only vegetable that is. One large carrot supplies an entire day's requirement of vitamin A, which is essential for healthy eyes, and thus explains the carrot's reputation of helping us to see in the dark.

1 If using fresh apricots, peel them following the instructions on page 15, then halve them, remove the stones, and peel away the skins.

2 Twist off the stalk from the pear, cut it into quarters, remove the core and peel.

3 Place the apricots and pear in a juicer, pour in half the carrot juice and blend until smooth. Add the rest of the carrot juice and blend again.

4 Skim or spoon off the froth, if preferred, pour into glasses and serve.

Dragon fruit blitz

With its vivid fuchsia-pink skin covered in large scales, the weird and wonderful dragon fruit certainly catches your eye if you spot it in exotic fruit markets alongside the more everyday melons and bananas. Also known as pitahaya and strawberry pear, dragon fruit is a member of the cactus family and, as well as the bright pink-skinned fruit with its white flesh and tiny black seeds that I've used here, you'll also find varieties that have horned yellow skin and deep purple-red flesh. Dragon fruit have been grown in Latin America since the time of the Aztecs in Peru. Now cultivated in many tropical areas, particularly in Asian countries like China, Vietnam and Indonesia, the flesh is mild and sweet and is a good source of fiber, vitamin C, and antioxidants.

1 Cut the dragon fruit in half lengthways and peel off the skin with a sharp knife. Cut the flesh into chunks.

2 Peel and chop the banana, peel the watermelon and pick out any seeds.

3 Put the dragon fruit, banana, and watermelon in a juicer, add the orange juice and grenadine and blend until smooth. Pour into glasses and serve at once.

INGREDIENTS

1 dragon fruit
1 small banana
6oz (175g) wedge of watermelon
1¼ cups (350ml) orange juice
2 tbsp grenadine syrup

TO SERVE

Scant 2/3 cup (5fl oz) heavy cream
½ tsp vanilla extract
Extra raspberries
Small mint leaves

MAKES

3¾ cups (900ml)

Green and go

Green bell peppers might not seem obvious candidates to go into a juice but they add their uniquely refreshing flavor and combine well with green grapes and honeydew melon, which add a touch of sweetness. Christopher Columbus is credited with introducing European palates to peppers, bringing them back from the Americas among his many fruit and vegetable discoveries. All bell peppers start life green before gradually turning red as they ripen, and although green peppers contain less vitamin C than red, pound for pound they have twice as much as oranges.

1 Remove the stalk and seeds from the bell pepper and cut the flesh into small pieces.

2 Pull the grapes off their stalks. Peel the melon, remove the seeds and cut the flesh into chunks.

3 Put the green pepper, grapes, and melon in a juicer and add the apple juice. Blend until smooth and, if you prefer to remove any small flecks of pepper or grape skin, strain the juice into glasses before serving.

INGREDIENTS

½ green pepper

6oz (175g) seedless green grapes

6oz (175g) wedge of honeydew melon

1¼ cups (300ml) apple juice

MAKES

2 cups (500ml)

Grapefruit, carrot, and ginger bliss

INGREDIENTS

2 medium carrots, total weight about
  5oz (150g)
½in (1cm) piece of root ginger
1 orange
1¼ cups (300ml) grapefruit juice
1–2 tbsp maple syrup, or to taste

MAKES

2½ cups (600ml)

Pungent and fiery but also warm and sweet, fresh ginger adds its own special lift to a juice. The root of the ginger plant, the spice has been grown in southeast Asia since the dawn of time but is now also cultivated in other areas of the world, including East Africa and the Caribbean islands. As well as its well-known culinary attractions, ginger has long been hailed for its medicinal qualities. Many pregnant women rely on ginger to curb morning sickness, it can help prevent the miseries of travel sickness, plus it eases digestion and stomach upsets and is an effective natural treatment for colds and coughs.

1 Peel the carrots and chop them into small pieces. Peel the ginger and grate or chop it finely.

2 Put the carrots and ginger in a small pan, add enough cold water to cover and simmer for 10 minutes or until the carrots are tender.

3 Drain, reserving ¼ cup of the cooking liquid and leave the carrots to cool.

4 Cut the rind and pith away from the orange and divide the flesh into segments.

5 Put the carrots and orange in a juicer with the reserved cooking liquid and blend until smooth. Add the grapefruit juice and maple syrup and blend again.

6 Pour into glasses and serve.

Long tall cooler

INGREDIENTS

12oz (350g) wedge of watermelon
4 tbsp crushed ice
¾ cup (175ml) pomegranate juice
2½ cups (600ml) sparkling apple juice

MAKES

4¼ cups (1 litre)

A long drink that's very refreshing on a hot day and is ideal for serving at a summer party. You could substitute ginger ale for the sparkling apple juice, or just sparkling mineral water; as an alternative to watermelon you could use the same weight of peaches, apricots, or papaya. To turn the cooler into a spritzer, replace half the apple juice with still or sparkling white wine.

1 Peel the watermelon, remove any seeds and cut the flesh into chunks.

2 Put the watermelon in a juicer with the crushed ice and pomegranate juice and blend until smooth.

3 Pour into tall glasses to roughly half-fill and top up with the sparkling apple juice.

4 Serve with a straw or stirrer in each glass and stir before drinking.

Lychee, strawberry, and grapefruit buzz

It's important to remove all the peel and pith from citrus fruit, as if these are blitzed with the other ingredients not only will they impart a bitter taste but fine threads of white pith may not break up completely and these will spoil the enjoyment of the finished juice. To prepare citrus fruits, trim a slice off the top and bottom of the fruit, then holding it upright, cut away the peel and pith in strips using a small serrated knife by starting at the top and working down to the base of the fruit. Cut out the segments of fruit, discarding the inner membrane holding them in place, but give the membrane a good squeeze to extract any remaining juice before discarding.

1 Cut the peel and white pith away from the grapefruit and divide the flesh into segments.

2 Peel the lychees and remove the stones. Hull the strawberries and halve or quarter any large fruits.

3 Put the grapefruit segments, lychees, and strawberries in a juicer and add the orange juice. Blend until smooth.

4 Pour into glasses and serve.

INGREDIENTS

1 pink or red grapefruit
8 lychees
5oz (150g) strawberries
1¾ cups (400ml) orange juice

MAKES

3 cups (700ml)

Kiwi, pineapple, and maple crush

If asked to name the fruit with the greatest levels of vitamin C, most of us would reply "oranges" but kiwi fruit actually contain twice as much of the sought-after vitamin and more fiber than apples. Looking like small, furry creatures with no heads, kiwi fruit never cease to delight when the brown skin is peeled away to reveal the vibrant emerald flesh with its tiny, jet-black seeds inside. Sweet, mild-flavored and juicy, mixed with other fruits they make a valuable contribution to all sorts of blended drinks.

1 Rub the rim of four glasses with the lime wedge. Mix a little powdered green food coloring, if using, with the sugar until it is evenly tinted, then spread out the sugar on a plate. Dip the rims of the glasses in the sugar to coat them in an even layer.

2 Peel and chop the kiwi fruit and cut the pineapple ring into small pieces.

3 Put the kiwi, pineapple, lime juice, maple syrup, and apple juice in a juicer and blend until smooth.

4 Pour into the glasses and serve at once.

INGREDIENTS

Lime wedge

Powdered green food coloring (optional)

3 tbsp superfine sugar

2 kiwi fruit

1 pineapple ring, fresh or canned

Juice of 2 limes

2 tbsp maple syrup

1¼ cups (300ml) apple juice

MAKES

2½ cups (600ml)

Kiwi, nectarine, and green grape juice

With skin as smooth and shiny as a peach skin's is matt and velvety, the nectarine is a close relative but is a fruit in its own right rather than a plum-peach hybrid. Sweet and juicy when ripe, they are usually smaller than peaches and can be white- or yellow-fleshed with either loose stones or ones that cling to the flesh. Nectarines have been cultivated in China for over 2,000 years but it wasn't until the late 16th century that they reached European shores. From there Spanish explorers took them to America, eventually transforming California into one of the nectarine-growing capitals of the world. High in antioxidants, nectarines are an excellent source of vitamin C as well as containing useful amounts of beta carotene, vitamin B, and potassium.

1 Peel the kiwi fruit and cut it into chunks.

2 Halve the nectarine, remove the stone and cut the flesh into thick slices. Pull the grapes off their stalks.

3 Put the kiwi fruit, nectarine, and grapes in a juicer and pour in the orange juice.

4 Blend until smooth. Strain through a fairly coarse sieve to remove any shreds of nectarine or grape skin and the kiwi seeds, if wished, or pour straight into glasses and serve.

INGREDIENTS

1 kiwi fruit
1 nectarine
8oz (225g) seedless green grapes
1¾ cups (400ml) orange juice

MAKES

3¾ cups (900ml)

Mango, coconut, and apple colada

INGREDIENTS

1 mango
1 small banana
¾ cup (200ml) apple juice
¾ cup (200ml) pineapple juice
½ cup (150ml) coconut milk

SERVES

Crushed ice or ice cubes

MAKES

3¾ cups (900ml)

Originally from south Asia where they have been cultivated for thousands of years, mangoes now grow in most frost-free tropical and sub-tropical climates. India is the number one producer of mangoes but only a tiny proportion of their crop finds its way into the world's fruit markets, as Indians eat most of what they grow themselves. The mango is India's national fruit and, unsurprisingly, of the 2,500-plus varieties that are found around the world, it is the Indian Alphonso that is the most highly prized. A medium-sized fruit, it has a yellow skin and deep orange flesh that is intensely flavored. Packed with vitamins, fiber, and powerful antioxidants, it's a pity not all foods that are "good for you" taste as seductive as mangoes.

1 Peel the mango and cut the flesh away from the fibrous centre stone.

2 Peel the banana and cut into chunks.

3 Put the mango, banana, and apple juice in a juicer and blend to a purée. Add the pineapple juice and coconut milk and blend again until smooth.

4 Pour into glasses over crushed ice or ice cubes and serve with a straw.

Mango and pineapple sunrise

Look for bottles of bright pink grenadine syrup amongst the drinks in larger supermarkets, or you can buy it from websites online. Made into a syrup from pomegranate juice, it contains no alcohol so can be added to drinks for both children and adults and only a splash is needed to give a juice a vibrant pinky-red hue. When making juices or smoothies, grenadine syrup can be added directly to the juicer with other fruits to enhance the overall color of the drink or, for a more striking effect, pour the drink into glasses before adding the grenadine. The latter will sink to the bottom of the glass and each drink will have its own rising—or setting—sun.

1 Peel the mango and cut the flesh away from the fibrous center stone using a sharp knife, holding the mango over a plate to collect any juice that runs out of it.

2 Put the mango flesh and its juice in a juicer, add the orange juice and pineapple juice and blend until smooth.

3 Pour into glasses and add a small splash of grenadine syrup to each. Leave until the grenadine sinks to the bottom of the glasses and swirl it into the drink with a skewer. Serve at once, decorating each glass with a wedge of fresh pineapple.

MERINGUES

1 medium mango, about 12oz (350g) unprepared weight
1 cup (250ml) orange juice
1¼ cups (300ml) pineapple juice

TO SERVE

Grenadine syrup and small pineapple wedges

MAKES

3¾ cups (900ml)

Mangosteen and watermelon refresher

Absolutely no relation to the mango, the mangosteen grows on a tropical, evergreen tree throughout southeast Asia. Its dark-purple, leathery skin gives no clue as to what lies beneath—delicate lychee-like flesh that is white and opaque with a sweet, tangy flavour and aroma. The skin is inedible so needs to be cut or pulled away to reveal the flesh that is divided into "petals," the largest of which contains a stubbornly attached stone that is well hidden. Although pleasant to eat, any significant health benefits of the mangosteen have yet to be proven, but beyond being said to aid digestion, the fruit does make a useful contribution to your daily intake of vitamin C.

1 Remove the stalk and cut the skin away from the mangosteen. Pull out the petals of flesh, removing the stone from the largest section.

2 Peel the papaya, remove the seeds and cut the flesh into chunks.

3 Peel the watermelon, pick out any seeds and cut the flesh into chunks.

4 Put the mangosteen flesh, papaya, and watermelon in a juicer, add the pineapple juice and blend until smooth.

5 Pour into glasses and serve.

INGREDIENTS

3 mangosteen
½ medium papaya
11oz (300g) wedge of watermelon
1¼ cups (300ml) pineapple juice

MAKES

3 cups (700ml)

INGREDIENTS

1 large orange

2 peaches, yellow or white fleshed

1½ cups (350ml) pineapple juice

MAKES

3 cups (700ml)

Peach perfect

"Just peachy," "you're a peach," and "everything's peaches 'n' cream" are just a few of the superlatives that owe their inspiration to one of the stars of the fruit world. An under-ripe a peach is hard and sharp-flavored and a sad shadow of the luscious yellow- or white-fleshed masterpiece it becomes when ripe. High in beta carotene, peaches aid digestion and help protect against lung and heart disease, but the main attraction is just eating them—or blending them to make a blissful juice.

1 Using a small, serrated knife, cut the peel and pith away from the orange and divide the flesh into segments.

2 Peel the peaches following the instructions on page 15, then cut them into quarters and remove the stones.

3 Place the orange segments and peaches in a juicer and pour in the pineapple juice. Blend until smooth, pour into glasses and serve.

Papaya, peach, and pineapple fizz

If you've been for a jog or finished a fierce workout at the gym and are feeling the effects, what you need is a big glassful of this juice as the sweet, fibrous flesh of pineapple contains bromelain, a natural enzyme that works its socks off to repair strained muscles and aching joints. When buying a pineapple, check that it feels heavy for its size and has a sweet, fragrant perfume. Under-ripe fruit are not only sharp-flavored and disappointing to eat, they also lack the all-important healing benefits. Once picked a pineapple won't ripen any more, so only buy fruit that's fully ripe.

INGREDIENTS

½ medium papaya, about 7oz (200g) in weight
1 yellow-fleshed peach
2 pineapple rings, fresh or canned in fruit juice
½ cup (150ml) orange juice

TO SERVE

Sparkling mineral water, well chilled

MAKES

1¾ cups (400ml) before the mineral water is added

1 Scoop the seeds out of the papaya, cut away the peel and chop the flesh.

2 Peel the peach following the instructions on page 15, then cut it into quarters, remove the stone and cut the flesh into thick slices.

3 Chop the pineapple rings into small pieces.

4 Put the papaya, peach, and pineapple in a juicer and add the orange juice. Blend until smooth.

5 Pour the fruit purée into glasses to half-fill them and top up with the sparkling mineral water. Serve at once.

Passion fruit sparkler

They might look like dirty purple golf balls but they say beauty is more than skin deep, and certainly the wrinklier the skin of a passion fruit, the juicier and more aromatic it will be. Grown on a vine that is native to Brazil, Paraguay, and northern Argentina, the seeds and pulp inside the fruit are high in beta carotene and vitamin C and are said to be good for anyone with high blood pressure. As well as purple passion fruit, there is also the maracuja or golden passion fruit that has an orangy-yellow smooth skin and is larger but more acidic than the purple variety.

1 Cut the passion fruit in half and scoop out the seeds and pulp into a small pan. Add the lemon juice and simmer for 2 minutes. Push through a sieve to separate the pulp from the seeds, discard the seeds and put the pulp in a juicer.

2 Peel the canteloupe melon and remove the seeds. Cut the flesh into chunks and add to the juicer with the pineapple juice and icing sugar.

3 Blend until smooth. Pour over ice cubes into glasses to half-fill and top up with soda water. Top each drink with a small wedge of canteloupe melon. Stir before drinking.

INGREDIENTS

6 passion fruit
1 tbsp lemon juice
½ canteloupe melon, weighing about 18oz (500g)
7fl oz (200ml) pineapple juice
1 tbsp icing sugar, or more to taste

TO SERVE

Ice cubes
Soda water
Small wedges of canteloupe melon

MAKES

3 cups (700ml) before being topped up with soda water

Melon and passion fruit glow

INGREDIENTS

4 passion fruit
2 cups (450ml) pineapple juice
¼ cantaloupe melon
1 small banana

MAKES

3½ cups (800ml)

Canteloupe melons have soft orange flesh with a musky aroma and when ripe they are lusciously sweet and juicy. The name "canteloupe" is French, derived from the original Italian name of Cantalupo, a former papal state near Rome where it is said the melons were first grown in Europe after being introduced there from the Middle East. Canteloupe melons belong to the same family as cucumbers, squashes, and pumpkins and contain useful amounts of vitamins A and C and potassium. The riper the melon, the sweeter it will be and also the more antioxidants it will contain.

1 Cut the passion fruit in half and scoop the seeds and pulp into a small pan. Add 2 tablespoons of the pineapple juice and heat gently for 2 minutes to help separate the seeds from the pulp. Push through a sieve, discard the seeds and put the pulp in a juicer.

2 Peel the melon, scoop out the seeds and chop the flesh. Peel the banana and cut the flesh into chunks.

3 Add the melon, banana, and the rest of the pineapple juice to the juicer and blend until smooth.

4 Pour into glasses and serve.

Peach, grape, and pineapple breeze

If you have a juicer with a powerful motor you can add ice cubes directly to the goblet to make crushed iced, but if you don't want to risk damaging your machine, the best way is to put ice cubes in a robust plastic bag, seal the top and bash them with a hammer to crush them into small pieces. It's a great way to release all those pent-up tensions after a frustrating day, but it's a job best undertaken on something sturdy, like a concrete floor.

1 Peel the peaches following the instructions on page 15, then halve them, remove the stones and cut the peaches into chunks or slices.

2 Pull the grapes off their stalks and place in a juicer. Add the peaches and half the pineapple juice and blend until smooth.

3 Sieve the purée to remove any small pieces of grape skin, if preferred. Return to the rinsed-out juicer, add the remaining pineapple juice and blend again.

4 Half-fill glasses with crushed ice and pour in the juice. Serve at once.

INGREDIENTS

2 peaches
6oz (175g) seedless red grapes
2 cups (500ml) pineapple juice

TO SERVE

Crushed ice

MAKES

4¼ cups (1 litre)

Pear, cucumber, and strawberry reviver

INGREDIENTS

1 pear
¼ cucumber
5oz (150g) strawberries
1½ cups (350ml) cranberry juice

MAKES

3½ cups (800ml)

For years the modest cucumber was regarded as a bit of a poor relation in the great superfoods family, being written off as a pleasant addition to salads and sandwiches but not much else. Admittedly the cucumber can't compete with the likes of avocados, broccoli, and spinach, but recently it has started to attract a more positive press. Cucumbers contain a useful amount of vitamins and minerals and their high water content helps keep the body hydrated. After tomatoes, cabbage, and onions, cucumbers are the fourth largest vegetable crop in the world, with cool green slices or sticks of it cropping up in virtually every cuisine. So while they might not be top of the superfood league, cucumbers don't lag behind in the popularity stakes.

1 Cut the pear into quarters, remove the stalk and core and peel away the skin.

2 Peel and deseed the cucumber and cut the flesh into chunks. Hull the strawberries and halve or quarter any large fruits.

3 Put the pear, cucumber, and strawberries in a juicer, add the cranberry juice and blend until smooth.

4 Pour into glasses and serve.

Pear, watercress, and melon cooler

INGREDIENTS

1 pear
6oz (175g) wedge of Ogen or Galia melon
1oz (25g) watercress
1½ cups (350ml) apple juice

MAKES

3 cups (700ml)

Watercress might not be everyone's favorite ingredient in a salad or sandwich, but included in a juice its bold, peppery flavor contrasts well with the sweetness of fruits like pear and melon, plus it gives the drink a beautiful jade green hue. In Ancient Greece when Hippocrates built the world's first hospital, he sited it by a freshwater stream so he had an abundant supply of watercress to speed his patients' recovery. Long regarded as one of nature's great protectors, its high levels of vitamin C helped overcome scurvy in the Middle Ages, while the Romans believed it cured madness—a claim that has yet to be proven!

1 Twist the stalk off the pear, cut it into quarters and remove the core. Peel away the skin and cut the flesh into chunks.

2 Peel the melon and discard the seeds. Pick any yellow leaves off the watercress and remove any tough stalks.

3 Put the pear, melon, and watercress in a juicer, pour in the apple juice and blend until smooth.

4 Strain or skim off any froth, if preferred, and pour into glasses.

Pear, cherry, and berry combo

Removing the pits from fresh cherries can be a boring job and although special pitting tools are available from kitchen shops, few of us pit enough cherries to make purchasing one worthwhile. The most efficient way to remove the pits is to cut round the cherries with a small, sharp knife, twist them in half and pick out the pits by hand, holding the fruit over the goblet of the juicer so you don't waste any juice that drips out.

1 Twist the stalk off the pear, cut it into quarters, remove the core and peel away the skin.

2 If using fresh cherries, pull them off their stalks and remove the pits.

3 Put the pear, cherries, and raspberries in a juicer, add the cranberry juice and honey and blend until smooth.

4 Strain, if preferred, to remove any flecks of cherry skin and the raspberry seeds, pour into glasses and serve. If left to stand the juice will separate, so pop a stirrer or swizzle stick in each glass.

INGREDIENTS

1 pear
5oz (115g) red cherries, fresh or canned (drained weight)
5oz (150g) raspberries
1½ cups (350ml) cranberry juice
1 tbsp honey, or to taste

MAKES

3 cups (700ml)

Lychee and papaya glow

INGREDIENTS

8 lychees
½ papaya, weighing about 11oz (300g)
Juice of 1 lime
½ cup (150ml) apple juice
1¼ cups (300ml) pineapple juice

MAKES

3 cups (750ml)

Sweet and fragrant, this juice owes much of its appeal to the aromatic lychees that go into it. Peel away the rough, brittle skin of a lychee and inside is a creamy white berry containing a shiny brown stone that is easily removed. Grown all over southeast Asia, the people of the north Thailand city of Chiang Rai are so proud of their lychees that each year they celebrate the start of the new season in mid-May with a special lychee festival, with beauty pageants, rows of stalls selling tempting food, and lots of partying. Lychees are a good source of vitamin C and also potassium, the latter helping nerves, blood pressure and the body's cells to work as they should.

1 Peel the lychees, run the point of a sharp knife around each fruit, open it up and remove the stone.

2 Peel the papaya, scoop out the black seeds and chop the flesh into chunks.

3 Put the lychees and papaya in a juicer, add the lime, apple, and pineapple juices and blend until smooth.

4 Pour into glasses and serve.

Pink cloud spritz

When goji (pronounced "go-gee") berries were first happened upon several years ago by intrepid seekers of new tastes, the tiny, brick-red berries were hailed as a miracle food, even being dubbed "fruit viagra." The jury seems to be out still on whether the slightly salty berries can actually deliver that result, but they do contain impressive amounts of vitamin C, beta carotene, and iron. The dried berries are expensive to buy but small cartons of goji berry juice are available—and more affordable. Only a little is needed to give this juice a healthy boost.

INGREDIENTS

1 pink grapefruit
¼ cup (50ml) goji berry juice
¾ cup (200ml) cranberry juice
2 tbsp maple syrup, or to taste
juice of 1 lime

TO SERVE

Sparkling mineral water and crushed ice
Lime wedges, to decorate

MAKES

1¾ cups (400ml) before the mineral water
 and ice are added

1 Peel the grapefruit, cutting away the skin and white pith with a sharp knife and divide into segments.

2 Put the grapefruit, goji berry juice, cranberry juice, maple syrup, and lime juice in a juicer and blend until smooth. Skim or strain off the frothy head, if preferred.

3 Pour into tall glasses over crushed ice to half-fill the glasses and top up with sparkling mineral water.

4 Tuck a lime wedge over the side of each glass and serve.

Pomelo and plum breeze

The giant of the citrus family, a pomelo can grow to 12in in diameter and weigh up to 25lb. Believed to be a relative of the grapefruit dating from way back, it is native to Malaysia but now also grown in Israel and California. An excellent source of vitamin C, potassium, and fiber, the pomelo is also one of the few fruits to contain calcium and protein. Its soft peel is very thick but easy to peel or cut away with a sharp knife, revealing pale yellow or coral-pink flesh inside. The flesh can vary from sweet to quite tart, so you may need to sweeten its juice with a little sugar or honey. As well as the health benefits of its flesh, the Chinese boil up pomelo peel and leaves to add to a ceremonial bath that is believed to cleanse the body of evil spirits.

1 Peel the pomelo, cutting away all the skin and pith. Divide the flesh into segments.

2 Remove the stalks from the plums, cut them in half and take out the stones.

3 Peel the melon, scrape away the seeds and cut the flesh into chunks.

4 Put the pomelo, plums, and melon in a juicer, add the apple and raspberry juice and blend until smooth.

5 Skim or spoon off the froth, if preferred, before pouring into glasses. Serve at once or with long spoons to give the drinks a good stir as the juice will separate.

INGREDIENTS

1 pomelo
8oz (225g) red-skinned plums
7oz (200g) wedge of honeydew melon
1¼ cups (300ml) apple and raspberry juice

TO SERVE

Sparkling mineral water and crushed ice,
* to serve*
Lime wedges, to decorate

MAKES

4¼ cups (1 litre)

Old-fashioned raspberry lemonade

They're one of our favorite berries but a mouthful of seeds in a drink, a coulis, or a dessert can be off-putting, so it's a good idea to sieve a raspberry purée before using it. Simmer the raspberries with liquid such as syrup or fruit juice as this will make it easier to push the purée through a sieve, and use the back of a spoon to extract as much juice from the pulp as possible.

INGREDIENTS

5oz (150g) superfine sugar
1 cup (225ml) water
1lb 2oz (500g) raspberries
4 large or 5 small lemons

TO SERVE

Sparkling mineral water
*Extra raspberries, lemon slices and mint
   sprigs, to decorate*

MAKES

*3¼ cups (800ml) before the mineral water
   is added*

1 Put the sugar and water in a pan and heat gently until the sugar dissolves, shaking and swirling the pan occasionally so grains of sugar don't stick to the bottom. Once the sugar has dissolved, bring the syrup to the boil then remove it from the heat and set it aside to cool completely.

2 Finely grate the zest from the lemons and squeeze out the juice—you will need almost 1 cup of lemon juice, so top up with extra juice if necessary.

3 Put the raspberries and lemon zest in a juicer, add the cooled syrup and lemon juice and blend to a purée.

4 Push the purée through a metal sieve to remove the raspberry pips and chill until ready to serve.

5 Give the raspberry purée a good stir as it will have separated. Pour into glasses to fill them by one-third and top up with sparkling water. Add extra raspberries, lemon slices, and mint sprigs to each glass and serve with straws.

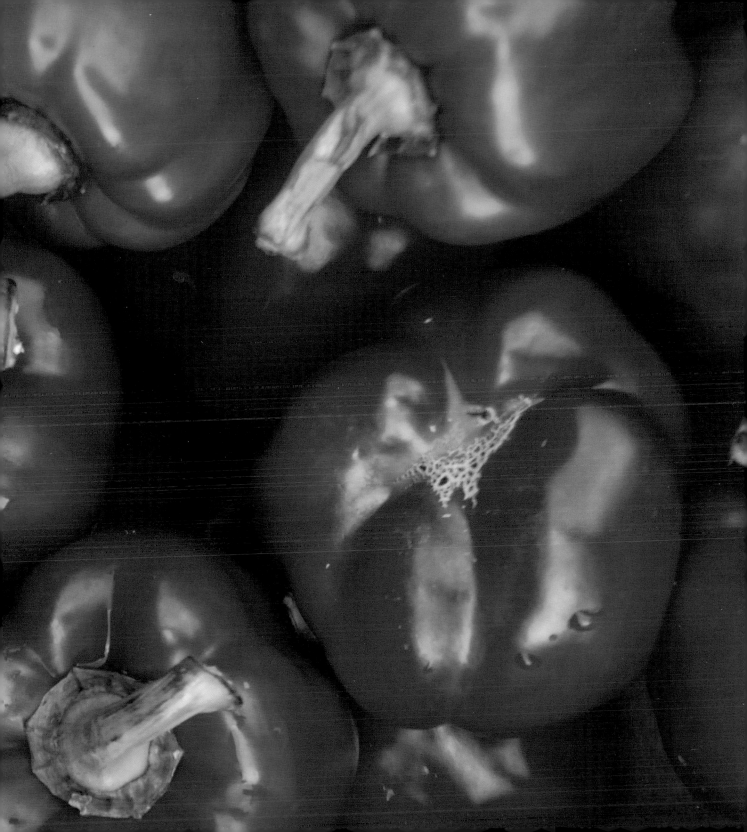

Red pepper wake-up call

Grilling the red bell pepper adds an extra dimension to the juice but, even though you're straining the pulp before you pour it into glasses, pull off the scorched pepper skin before you toss it into the juicer or the very subtle, slightly smoky flavor of the juice could turn from soft and mellow to burnt! The finished juice can be sprinkled with golden linseeds (also known as flaxseeds) which may look tiny and insignificant but are in fact a nutritional powerhouse. High in fiber, their healthy credentials extend to including nature's answer to HRT, due to their high content of the plant chemicals known as phytoestrogens that boost oestrogen levels in the female body.

1 Line a grill pan with foil, place the red bell pepper on it and grill until the skin is scorched and blackened all over, turning the pepper over occasionally so it colors evenly. Wrap the foil around the pepper and leave until it is cool enough to unwrap the pepper and peel off the skin. Halve, remove the stalk and seeds and cut the flesh into chunks.

2 Peel the carrots and chop into small pieces. Simmer in a pan of boiling water until tender. Drain and leave to cool.

3 Pull the grapes off their stalks and put in a juicer with the pepper and carrots.

4 Add the orange juice and blend until smooth. Strain into glasses and serve sprinkled with golden linseeds. As the juice separates, serve with spoons or straws to stir it up.

INGREDIENTS

1 red pepper

2 medium carrots

3oz (75g) seedless red grapes

1½ cups (350ml) orange juice

TO SERVE

Golden linseeds

MAKES

2½ cups (600ml)

Red berry and bitter lemon soda

Glistening like bright jewels on a necklace or brooch, redcurrants are another winner in the good health-promoting stakes. Rich in fiber and vitamin C, they have been credited with a whole raft of benefits that range from reducing fever and cleansing the blood, to acting as a mild laxative. Unfortunately, like their close cousin the gooseberry, eating the pretty little currants on their own can be a bit of a let down, as redcurrants have little distinguishing flavor to make them stand out and they can be rather sharp for many tastes. Blended with sweeter berries to make a juice or smoothie, however, redcurrants come into their own, adding not just color but also balancing sweeter fruit with a welcome tartness.

1 Hull the strawberries and quarter or halve any large fruits.

2 Pull the redcurrants from their stalks and put in a juicer with the strawberries and raspberries.

3 Add the orange juice and honey and blend until smooth.

4 Strain through a sieve into a jug to remove the raspberry seeds and gradually stir in the bitter lemon or lemonade.

5 Pour into glasses and decorate each drink with small redcurrant sprigs.

INGREDIENTS
6oz (175g) strawberries
4oz (115g) redcurrants
4oz (115g) raspberries
1–2 tbsp honey, or to taste
Freshly squeezed juice of 1 orange
1¾ cups (400ml) bitter lemon or traditional sparkling lemonade

TO SERVE
Redcurrant sprigs

MAKES
3¼ cups (800ml)

Spinach, apple, and grape boost

INGREDIENTS

1oz (25g) young spinach leaves
¼ cucumber
3oz (75g) seedless green grapes
1 apple
1½ cups (350ml) orange juice

TO SERVE

Fine sticks of cucumber

MAKES

3¼ cups (800ml)

Popeye the sailor man has put spinach on the map for generations of cartoon lovers, and as it is bursting with vitamin C, iron, and beta carotene, there's no disputing its body building credentials. In addition, the deep green leaves are packed with oxygen-boosting chlorophyll, plus they are a good source of fiber. On the down side, spinach does contain high levels of oxalic acid, which if eaten in large quantities interferes with the body's capacity to absorb calcium, so when making a juice the leaves need to be mixed with other vegetables or fruit.

1 Remove any tough stalks from the spinach leaves and shred the leaves.

2 Peel the cucumber, remove the seeds and chop the flesh into chunks. Pull the grapes off their stalks.

3 Quarter, core, and peel the apple.

4 Put the spinach leaves, cucumber, grapes, and apple in a juicer and add the orange juice. Blend until smooth.

5 Pour into glasses and serve with fine sticks of cucumber tucked into each drink.

Strawberry, apple, and red grape treat

When strawberries are out of season and imported fruit lacks the luscious sweetness of homegrown berries, you can make this juice using frozen fruit. Don't bother to defrost the strawberries, just tip them into the juicer while still frozen, blend with the apple and grape juice and you'll have deliciously long and cooling drink.

1 Hull the strawberries and cut any large fruits into halves or quarters.

2 Quarter, core, and peel the apple. Cut into chunks and put in a juicer with the strawberries and red grape juice.

3 Blend until smooth. Skim or spoon off excess froth, if preferred, then pour into glasses and serve.

INGREDIENTS
6oz (175g) strawberries
1 apple
1¼ cups (300ml) red grape juice

MAKES
3 cups (700ml)

Strawberry, lime, and cherry cola

If asked to vote for their favorite fruit, strawberries would be top of many people's list. Before the 17th century all European strawberries were tiny, wild, Alpine berries that were eaten partly for pleasure but also because they were prized for their ability to break down uric acid in the body, the painful results of which in the form of gout and kidney stones were most likely due to latter-day gourmets' over-indulgence in rich foods. The larger berries we enjoy today are descended from two American varieties and strawberries still have the reputation of easing painful joints, as well as containing high levels of vitamin C and soluble fiber to help lower cholesterol.

1 Hull the strawberries and quarter or halve any large fruits.

2 Remove the stalks and stones from the cherries.

3 Put the strawberries, cherries, lime juice, and apple juice in a juicer and blend until smooth.

4 Strain into a jug, if preferred, to remove any small shreds of cherry skin and skim or spoon off any froth. Top up with the cola.

5 Pour into tall glasses over crushed ice or ice cubes and serve with extra strawberries.

INGREDIENTS

6oz (175g) strawberries
4oz (115g) red cherries
Juice of 1 lime
½ cup (150ml) apple juice

TO SERVE

330ml can cola
crushed ice or ice cubes
extra strawberries

MAKES

3 cups (700ml)

Strawberry and redcurrant delight

INGREDIENTS

5oz (150g) redcurrants
6oz (175g) strawberries
½ cup (150ml) white grape juice
2½ cups (600ml) sparkling mineral water

MAKES

3¼ cups (750ml) before the sparkling
*   mineral water, if added*

Look for cartons of white grape juice that haven't been sweetened, as the natural sweetness of 100% juice combined with the strawberries provides the perfect balance in this drink. Reputed to cure migraines if drunk neat first thing in the morning, white grape juice also replenishes stocks of iron in the body and fights tiredness. As it is so easy to digest, recent medical research points to it being a suitable first juice to introduce into the diet of toddlers and babies over six months old.

1 Strip the redcurrants from their stalks and place in a juicer.

2 Hull the strawberries and halve or quarter any large fruits.

3 Add the strawberries to the juicer with the white grape juice and blend until smooth.

4 Divide the strawberry purée between glasses and top up with the mineral water. Serve as soon as the excess bubbles settle down.

Tokyo Virgin Mary

The innocent little sister of a Bloody Mary, but of course grownups can add a good slug of vodka or sake for something a bit more fortifying, while consoling themselves that they're still getting the benefit of that powerhouse of antioxidants, lycopene, in the tomatoes. Wasabi paste is a fiery green Japanese horseradish that looks deceptively innocuous when you squeeze it from its toothpaste-like tube, but unless you truly like things hot, it's best to err on the side of caution. After all, you can always add more.

1 Peel the cucumber and remove the seeds.

2 Pull the grapes off their stalks and place in a juicer with the cucumber.

3 Add the tomato juice, mirin, wasabi paste, and soy sauce and blend until smooth.

4 Strain to remove any debris from the grapes and pour into glasses over ice cubes. Serve garnished with sticks of cucumber.

INGREDIENTS
¼ cucumber
5oz (150g) seedless green grapes
1¼ cups (300ml) tomato juice
½ cup (150ml) apple juice
1 tbsp mirin or another sweet rice wine
½–1 tsp wasabi paste, or to taste
Dash of Japanese soy sauce

TO SERVE
Ice cubes and cucumber sticks

MAKES
2½ cups (600ml)

Watermelon and strawberry buzz

Few fruits look as dramatic when you cut into them as watermelon, with their dark green skin, glistening scarlet flesh and tiny black seeds. The flesh is sublime to eat—sweet, refreshing and dripping with juice—but what is less well known is that the skin is edible too and contains many nutrients. Unsurprisingly, most people don't fancy chewing on a chunk of the tough green rind, so the good news is the flesh contains its fair share of nutrients too, including large amounts of beta carotene and lycopene. Watermelons are thought to be native to southern Africa, where they grow wild, but their fame obviously spread north as watermelon seeds have been found in the tomb of Tutankhamun.

1 Peel the watermelon. Pick out and discard any seeds and cut the flesh into chunks.

2 Hull the strawberries and cut any large ones into halves or quarters.

3 Put the watermelon and strawberries in a juicer, add the grape juice and blend until smooth.

4 Skim or strain off any excess froth, if preferred, and pour the juice into glasses. Serve with small wedges of watermelon and strawberries to enjoy with the juice.

INGREDIENTS

14oz (400g) slice of watermelon
5oz (150g) strawberries
1¼ cups (300ml) white grape juice

TO SERVE

Extra watermelon wedges and strawberries

MAKES

3 cups (700ml)

Light my fire

Is there anything that can't have a ubiquitous chilli added to it these days? Well, if chillies can be added to ice cream and chocolate mousse, the answer is probably "no," as here it's even crept into an otherwise innocuous-looking juice. We all know that chillies are good for us, whether we need our tubes cleared when we're bunged up with a cold, our metabolism sent into overdrive so we burn more fat, or our immune system boosted to ward off winter bugs. However, not everyone likes feeling the heat, so while chilli adds its own special kick to this juice, do leave it out if you prefer. And, remember, the smaller the chilli, the hotter it's likely to be, so choose your chilli with care.

INGREDIENTS

9oz (250g) tomatoes, about 3 medium
1 large orange
1¼ cups (300ml) carrot juice
ice cubes or crushed ice
½ red chilli, deseeded and very finely chopped

TO SERVE

Fine shreds of red chilli and carrot curls

MAKES

2½ cups (600ml)

1 Put the tomatoes in a heatproof bowl, pour over boiling water to cover and leave them to stand for 45 seconds. Drain into a sieve and run cold water over the tomatoes until they are cool enough to handle. Remove any stalks, cut the tomatoes into quarters, peel off the skins, and scoop out and discard the seeds.

2 Cut the peel and pith away from the orange and divide into segments.

3 Put the tomato flesh and orange segments in a juicer, add the carrot juice and blend until smooth. Taste to see if you need to add more chilli and, if so, add the desired amount and blend again.

4 Put a few ice cubes or a couple of tablespoons of crushed ice in each glass. Strain the froth off the juice, if preferred, and pour into the glasses.

5 Decorate each drink with fine shreds of red chilli and carrot curls. To make carrot curls, shave off thin slices of carrot lengthways using a vegetable peeler. Cut the slices into thin strips, place in a bowl of cold water and chill until the strips curl.

Spinach and honeydew breeze

A ripe honeydew is the sweetest and most nutritious of the melon family, its pale green flesh being tender, succulent, and deliciously juicy. The flesh is rich in vitamin C, potassium, folate, and vitamin B6, all of which help lower blood pressure, aid circulation, and relieve skin disorders. When buying a honeydew melon, the easiest way to tell if it is ripe is to pick it up and smell it. If it has a fragrant, honeyed aroma that is how it will taste. If it has no scent at all, it is unlikely to taste of much either.

1 Remove any stalks from the spinach and coarsely shred the leaves.

2 Peel and deseed the cucumber and cut into chunks.

3 Peel the melon, discard the seeds and cut the flesh into chunks.

4 Put the spinach, cucumber, and melon into a juicer, add the apple juice and blend until smooth, stopping the machine once or twice to push down any shreds of spinach that stick to the sides of the goblet.

5 Skim or strain off any froth on the surface, if preferred, pour into glasses and serve. After a while the juice will separate, so stir it up before serving, if necessary.

INGREDIENTS

2oz (50g) young spinach leaves
¼ cucumber
14oz (400g) wedge of honeydew melon
1¾ cups (400ml) apple juice

MAKES

3¾ cups (900ml)

Index